C000117912

BARCELONA

here we come!

THE STORY OF RANGERS' EUROPEAN CUP WINNERS CUP WIN 1972

RONNIE ESPLIN &
ALEX ANDERSON
PHOTOGRAPHS BY ERIC MCCOWAT

publishing

For Kirsty, Alexander and Mhairi,
who continue to inspire.
Ronnie Esplin

For my Dad, the John Greig of the
Anderson team.
Alex Anderson

© Ronnie Esplin & Alex Anderson 2002
© Photographs Eric McCowat

First published in 2002 by
Argyll Publishing
Glendaruel
Argyll PA22 3AE
Scotland
under Licence from The Rangers
Football Club plc

The authors have asserted their moral
rights.

**British Library Cataloguing-in-
Publication Data.
A catalogue record for this book is
available from the British Library.**

ISBN 1 902831 37 3

Layout & design Michael Kaufman
Typeset in Garamond 10/15

Printing Cromwell Press

CONTENTS

Acknowledgements   3

1 Introduction   5

2 Season 1971/72
   – the background   11

3 The Journey Begins
   – Rennes   19

4 Sporting Lisbon   29

5 Torino   43

6 Bayern Munich   61

7 The Final
   Rangers v Moscow Dynamo   75

8 'Madness Breaks Out'   97

9 Epilogue   107

Notes   115

References   124

Rangers' European record
   to 1971/72   125

Front Cover picture
Rangers striker Colin Stein fights for
the ball against a Moscow Dynamo
defender in the Barcelona final of the
1972 European Cup Winners Cup. This
is clearly second half action since the
players changed their commemorative
shirts at half time.
Back cover
The Rangers squad two months later in
their pre-season photo 1972/73

ACKNOWLEDGEMENTS

The authors would like to thank the following people who contributed in various ways to the making of this book. Paul Geddes of Rangers helped set the ball rolling and we must of course thank a number of the central characters of the '71/'72 side, Willie Johnston, Colin Jackson, Sandy Jardine, Colin Stein, Tommy McLean, Peter McCloy and Alex MacDonald who spared their time to speak to us. The pleasure was ours.

The French connection came from the enthusiastic Greg Pichet. Phil Town researched and translated important sections of the Sporting chapter and our Italian contacts Marco Masoero, Mauro Ricci and Ruth Trotter could not have been more helpful. We thank them all. We are also grateful to Uli Hesse-Lichtenberger, Derek O'Rourke and Antje Haertel for help with the German section.

In the spirit of *glasnost*, Moscow Dynamo FC's former press officer Oleg B Medvedev helped enormously with important initial contacts, spellings and translations. Sergei Markov and Ded Borsov also helped with translations and were bountiful in their anecdotes and Katia Rogatchevskaia's help in the early days was crucial.

Jordi Rosiboro gave up his valuable time in the Barcelona sunshine to advise, inform and entertain and Morag Ramsay's Spanish and French translations were invaluable. Archie McPherson must also be thanked for his recollections of both the Old Firm's European triumphs. A big thanks to Rangers fans Billy McMahon, Garry Lynch, Jim Shirkie, John Powell, John Miller and Jack Bain all of whom kindly shared their recollections of what, clearly, was a memorable time for all concerned.

Welcome advice and encouragement came from Colin Glass, Bill Murray, Graham Walker, George Wells, David Low, Andy Lyons, Craig Ellyard, Adam Powley, Scott Danks, Jeremy Troy and Andrew Inglis. Thanks once again to publisher Derek Rodger for all his help and advice.

Special mentions:

To Howard and Louise Cardwell for introducing me to the beautiful obsessions – Rangers and European football. And most of all, to Hilary, for absolutely everything.   Alex Anderson

To Brendan Bradley of Cambuslang College for instilling confidence and belief.   Ronnie Esplin
                                                               March 2002

1

INTRODUCTION

The Rangers party set off for the final in Barcelona 1972
Back Standing (l to r) Fyfe, Johnston, McCloy, Miller (crouching), Parlane,
Johnstone, Conn, Neef, MacDonald, Watson, Greig, Smith, Penman
Front (l to r) Stein, McLean, Denny, Mathieson (Sandy Jardine is last off the
plane)

Barcelona – here we come!

'History has struggled to classify Barcelona '72'

On the 24th May 1972, in the most dramatic of evenings in Barcelona, Glasgow Rangers defeated Moscow Dynamo 3-2 to win the European Cup Winners Cup. It was a night never to be forgotten – in more ways than one – and marked the end of a peculiar and sometimes bizarre campaign which, three decades later, demands renewed interpretation and evaluation.

Rangers' successful European season must rank as one of the most intriguing, fascinating and downright puzzling in any football club's history. The triumph was neither predicted nor expected because, unlike most European trophy winners, this was not a team on the crest of a wave. In fact, the Ibrox club were arguably in the doldrums, having won only one trophy, a League Cup, in the previous five seasons as they fell further behind their powerful rivals Celtic.[1] Indeed, Rangers had suffered the ignominy of qualifying for the Cup Winners Cup only as beaten finalists to the Parkhead side in the Scottish Cup.

The early season signs were not encouraging and 'crisis at Ibrox' calls came only weeks into the campaign as Rangers flirted with the bottom of the 18-team Scottish First Division. Although they eventually climbed back up the table, a relatively poor domestic season ensued, compounded by a whitewashing from Celtic in their four meetings in the League and League Cup. It was, obviously, not a situation conducive to European success. However, this Rangers side tore up the script when turning in nine performances of determination, courage, discipline and skill to bring back a European trophy to Ibrox for the first time.

History has struggled to classify Barcelona '72. The players who battled to victory in the Nou Camp have never quite found their place in Ibrox folklore or indeed in the overall Scottish football mosaic.[2] For most football teams and their fans, the winning of a European trophy is the high point in a club's history. From that day, legends are born and this was certainly the case for the two other Scottish clubs who have captured European trophies, Celtic and Aberdeen.[3] Their successes, however, were more straightforward. Both clubs won their respective European trophies with their best ever sides. This was patently not the case with Rangers.

There have long been arguments amongst Rangers fans concerning which of the Ibrox sides have been 'The Best'. The Barcelona side seldom figures. The Greig-McKinnon-Baxter era of the early sixties, the treble-winning teams of 1976 and 1978 which contained a core of the Barcelona troops and the powerful and talented early 1990s' Rangers side, all have their devotees. As successful as these teams undoubtedly were, they all have one thing in common – they didn't win a European trophy.

So how did the team of '71/'72 manage this success in Europe? It certainly wasn't easy. The road to

Rangers confined their inconsistency to the Scottish domestic scene. In the first round of the Cup Winners Cup, French side Rennes, although an unknown quantity, provided a stiff opening test. However, a 1-1 draw away from home followed by a 1-0 win at Ibrox was enough to see the Scots through. But

the penalty charade in Lisbon

Barcelona was undoubtedly a tough journey and each of the Ibrox men's opponents, whose qualities and status ranged from highly competent to fearsome, posed different challenges and problems. There were certainly no sacrificial lambs offered up for the Rangers team of '72 – but how could there have been given the Ibrox side's erratic league form? How can a team, between defeating the Bayern Munich of Beckenbauer and Muller and beating Moscow Dynamo in the Nou Camp, lose at home to bottom of the table Dunfermline?

That season, fortuitously, because we must presume it wasn't planned,

they made few friends in Brittany with the power and commitment needed to compensate for their early-season lack of confidence.

In the next round came the infamous drama in the return leg of the Sporting Lisbon tie. After winning 3-2 at Ibrox, Rangers lost by the same margin in Portugal. A goal apiece in extra time flummoxed the referee who went through a penalty charade which Rangers lost spectacularly – missing their first four spot kicks! However, the momentary panic for Rangers and their fans dissolved when the rule book confirmed that away goals in extra time did indeed count double. Over the two

Barcelona – here we come!

free-flowing ties, which resembled nothing like the archetypal strategic 'chess matches' of European competition, it was a deserved victory for the Scots and unlike the previous round, the Ibrox players impressed with their verve, skill and ability.

In the quarter-finals, Rangers faced up to Italian side Torino, at that time as equally talented and famous as their city neighbours Juventus. Both Turin sides, coincidentally, were fighting out a fierce championship battle which prompted claims that, with one eye on the *Scudetto*, and an upcoming derby game, the Italians fielded a weakened team at Ibrox in the second leg. But Italian teams are historically formidable, and unsurprisingly, the two matches were tight and hard fought. In the end, after a 1-1 first leg draw in Italy, Rangers slipped through to the semi-finals with a one-goal win at Ibrox. European glory, hitherto an unlikely proposition, was now firmly fixed in the Ibrox sightlines.

The Turin side could hardly have posed more of a problem than the mighty Bayern Munich whose players were in the early years of German, European and World football domination. The Bavarians were old foes. They had beaten Rangers in the 1967 European Cup Winners Cup final, in what was effectively a home game in Nuremberg, and had triumphed against them again more recently, in the 1970/71 Fairs Cities Cup. The Ibrox men could have been excused for thinking

Alex MacDonald accompanies the ball into the net for his goal against Torino

the end of the continental road had been reached. But with determination, spirit and no little skill, Rangers survived a difficult first leg tie to escape from Germany with a 1-1 draw before winning 2-0, somewhat easily. In front an incredulous but ecstatic 80,000 fans at Ibrox.

With confidence brimming, despite a poor end to the league campaign, the Ibrox men, followed by thousands of 'de-mob happy' supporters, arrived in Barcelona to take on the Russians of Moscow Dynamo. Both sides had famously clashed in Dynamo's post-war tour of Britain and had coincidentally met at Ibrox in a friendly the previous season. But this was different, this was Rangers' date with destiny, the end of a long quest for European glory. In what was a glorious yet tainted night of football, Rangers almost snatched defeat from the jaws of victory in a game of high drama and excitement. Focused, determined and spirited, the Ibrox men raced into a 3-0 lead only to run out of steam, conceding two second-half, panic-inducing goals. But Willie Waddell's men held on grimly for victory and only the most mean-spirited would deny that Rangers deserved their success. Few, however, would have predicted that the victory represented the beginning of the end for Scottish clubs as a force in European football.[4]

The intervening years have seen the Barcelona success all but ignored and there has been little of substance written or recorded about the campaign. There are several reasons for this apparent indifference, one being that it didn't compare with the historic nature of Celtic's 1967 win in Lisbon, a momentous event in British football which cast a permanent shadow over Ibrox. And in a purely Scottish context, Rangers' success lacked the provincial romance of Aberdeen's successful campaign of 1982/83. Moreover, the triumph, difficult as it was, came immediately on the back of English success in the same competition thus diluting the novelty of the achievement.

Perhaps more significantly, there is also the small matter of the post-match pitch invasion which was, and arguably still is, the normal means of celebrating such a momentous victory. However, to the eternal embarrassment and frustration of Rangers Football Club and their fans, circumstances meant that a joyous event turned sour. Regardless of who was to blame, the ugly riot which ensued prevented the symbolic trophy presentation to captain John Greig and thus robbed the night of much of the glory associated with a European victory. All these contributory factors, compounded by the one-season ban from European competition, combined to push Barcelona '72 out of the limelight.

However, despite the ambiguity surrounding the standing of Rangers' European Cup Winners Cup victory, a story is there to be told and thirty years on, this book, with the help of players, fans and the media, catalogues and puts in context the extraordinary journey from Rennes to Barcelona.

Of course the potential problem with commemorative books is that they can slide head-first into myopic sentimentality, where even the most workmanlike players gain God-like status, flawed teams become invincible, and narrow, hard-fought and arguably lucky victories become heroic triumphs of adventurous attacking football. We hope this has been resisted. This is an honest attempt to capture the spirit and essence of what is that rarest of sporting events, a Scottish football club winning a European trophy.

Barcelona – here we come!

RANGERS 1971/72 SEASON

Jul 20 (A) G.A.I.S. Gothenburg (Fr) L 3-4
(Gothenburg Alliance Jubilee Tournament)
Jul 21 (A) Orgryte I.S. (Fr) W 4-2
Jul 26 (A) Helsingborgs I.F. (Fr) W 4-0

Aug 6 (H) Everton (Fr) W 2-1
Aug 9 (H) Tottenham H (Fr) W 1-0
Aug 14 (A*) Celtic (SLC) L 0-2
*played at Ibrox
Aug 18 (H) Ayr United (SLC) W 4-0
Aug 21 (H) Morton (SLC) W 2-0
Aug 25 (A) Ayr United (SLC) W 4-0
Aug 28 (H) Celtic (SLC) L 0-3

Sept 1 (A) Morton (SLC) W 1-0
Sept 4 (A) Partick Thistle L 2-3
Sept 11 (H) Celtic L 2-3
Sept 15 (A) Rennes D 1-1
Sept 18 (A) Falkirk W 3-0
Sept 25 (H) Aberdeen L 0-2
Sept 28 (H) Rennes W 1-0

Oct 2 (A) Hearts L 1-2
Oct 9 (H) East Fife W 3-0
Oct 16 (A) Dundee Utd W 5-1
Oct 20 (H) S.Lisbon W 3-2
Oct 23 (H) Motherwell W 4-0
Oct 30 (H) Kilmarnock W 3-1

Nov 3 (A) S.Lisbon L 3-4
Nov 6 (A) St.Johnstone W 4-1
Nov 13 (H) Dundee L 2-3
Nov 20 (A) Morton W 2-1
Nov 24 (A) Chelsea (Fr) W 1-0
Nov 27 (A) Ayr Utd W 2-1

Dec 4 (H) Clyde W 1-0
Dec 7 (A) Hapoel/Maccabbi Tel Aviv
Select (Fr) D 0-0

Dec 11 (A) Dunfermline W 2-0
Dec 18 (H) Airdrie W 3-0
Dec 25 (A) Hibs W 1-0

Jan 1 (H) Partick Th W 2-1
Jan 3 (A) Celtic L 1-2
Jan 8 (H) Falkirk W 3-1
Jan 15 (A) Aberdeen D 0-0
Jan 22 (H) Hearts W 6-0
Jan 29 (A) East Fife W 1-0

Feb 5 (A) Falkirk (SC) D 2-2
Feb 9 (H) Falkirk (SC) W 2-0
Feb 12 (H) Dundee Utd W 1-0
Feb 19 (A) Motherwell L 0-2
Feb 26 (A) St Mirren (SC) W 4-1

Mar 4 (A) Kilmarnock W 2-1
Mar 8 (A) Torino D 1-1
Mar 11 (H) St Johnstone W 2-0
Mar 18 (A) Motherwell (SC) D 2-2
Mar 22 (H) Torino W 1-0
Mar 25 (H) Morton L 1-2
Mar 27 (H) Motherwell (SC) W 4-2

Apr 5 (A) Bayern Munich D 1-1
Apr 8 (A) Clyde D 1-1
Apr 10 (A) Dundee L 0-2
Apr 15 (N) Hibs (SC) D 1-1
Apr 19 (H) Bayern Munich W 2-0
Apr 22 (A) Airdrie W 3-0
Apr 24 (N) Hibs (SC) L 0-2
Apr 27 (H) Dunfermline L 3-4
Apr 29 (H) Hibs L 1-2

May 1 (H) Ayr Utd W 4-2
May 10 (A) Inverness Select (Fr) W 5-2
May 16 (A) ST Mirren (Fr) W 5-2
May 24 (N) Moscow Dynamo W 3-2

Barcelona – here we come!

'The vital issue for Rangers in the new season - more than anything we want to win that flag.'
Willie Waddell

As preparations for season 1971/72 were being made, some familiar concerns about Scottish football were heard. The historical dominance of the Old Firm was, unsurprisingly, on the agenda although the gap between them and the rest of the teams wasn't quite the chasm it is at present. In fact, as far as struggling Rangers were concerned the gap was barely discernible.

In addition to on-field problems, the Govan club were still coming to terms with the Ibrox disaster in which 66 fans had died in a stairway crush at the end of an Old Firm game.

Celtic were the dominant of the two Glasgow sides and were embarking on a quest for their seventh league title in a row. Indeed, such was the Parkhead side's superiority over their city rivals that Rangers' League Cup win over the champions the previous season was heralded with an excitement and joy that young Ibrox fans would find bemusing. But in a time of desperation, any straw was worth clutching.

With Celtic so monotonously successful – their crowds actually went down as the league flags and trophies piled up – the calls for league restructuring could have been borrowed from modern day complainants. Overall in Scotland, attendances had dropped from their post-war peak although, Old Firm attendances apart, they were relatively booming in comparison with the present SPL crowd levels.

It was certainly a more parochial era. The League Championship was still the main goal of the Old Firm at the outset of every season and the domestic cups still enjoyed a decent amount of prestige. There wasn't the financial pressure to succeed on the European stage which nowadays consumes Glasgow's big two and there was no serious talk, from clubs, fans or media about European 'Super leagues' although the idea of Rangers and Celtic moving to England was a recurrent theme. European football was regarded, to use a cliché, as the, 'icing on the cake'.

The terracing culture of pay-at-the-gate, 'lift overs' for children, carry-outs, pies and Bovril, standing in the rain and snow and hazardous toilet 'arrangements' had continued practically unchanged for almost a century. Season tickets, although restricted by football legislation, were only for the well-heeled and were way down the aspiration list of the ordinary fan. Significantly, not having paid a large fee in advance, it allowed supporters to pick and choose their games and as a consequence attendance figures varied widely from match to match.

Fans knew little about foreign football. Interest in such matters only awoke in World Cup years, with the European Championships a mere shadow of the event it is today. National boundaries remained strong and in the main Scottish club sides comprised eleven Scotsmen with the overseas player plying his trade in Scotland the exception rather than the rule. Rangers were no different and in season 1971/72 reserve goalkeeper Gerry Neef was the only foreigner at Ibrox and he rarely played first team football. By contrast, in season 2001/2002 Barry Ferguson was often the only Scotsman in the starting eleven.

The press had had a long relationship with football but they and the media in general were less pervasive and powerful than today. The football authorities in Scotland ruled with an iron rod and there was a long history of antagonism towards live television and radio coverage, although the latter was deemed slightly less evil. The notion that broadcasters should provide fans with as much televised football as they wanted simply wasn't on the agenda and looking at it from the perspective of modern day saturation, it seems remarkable that the first Scottish Cup final to be shown live on television was in 1977. The term 'armchair fan' had little relevance. In those pre-Sky Sports days, when fans had yet to metamorphose into full-blown consumers, supporters were restricted to grudging highlights programmes such as *Match Report* or *Sportsreel* and the occasional live broadcast was to be cherished.

Newspaper editors were slowly emerging from a decades-long love-in with the Ibrox club and criticisms began to find their way onto the front pages, but in terms of the sports desks the reporters generally had a more amicable and mutually beneficial relationship with football managers. In some cases they had little option. Broadcaster Archie Macpherson recalled that Celtic manager Jock Stein would manipulate the press to his own ends and 'would virtually dictate the copy that certain writers put in'. [1]

The intense marketing of football was in its infancy but it appears that advertising rates in the early 1970s were favourable for clubs. The first Old Firm fixture of the 1971/72 season, unsurprisingly sold-out, was advertised in the *Daily Record* on the day of the game! Was it thought that Rangers and Celtic fans might perhaps have overlooked it? Although arguably even more bizarre were the adverts for Partick Thistle reserve games which appeared regularly throughout the season. [2]

The financial implications of being a football fan didn't dominate pub conversations. The game was affordable for the supporters – still mainly the traditional working class – and admission prices were less prohibitive than at present. Main Stand tickets for Rangers' European home tie against

Sporting Lisbon were £1 and £1.50, enclosure 50p and ground admission was 30p. The Old Firm reserve game at Parkhead could be accessed for the princely sum of 30p for the Main Stand, 15p for the terracing and seven and a half pence for boys and OAPs. [3]

The national team, equal to club sides in terms of importance and interest generated, were also inexpensive to support. Scotland could attract attendances as high as anywhere in the world.[4] The friendly against Portugal at Hampden that season, watched by an incredible 58,000 spectators, was a case in point. The all-ticket Main Stand was priced at £1.50 with the North Enclosure and covered terracing (Rangers end) at 40p.[5] The huge Hampden crowd was indicative of the national team's standing. Unlike nowadays, Old Firm fans and Rangers fans in particular, were passionate and enthusiastic about the Scottish national team. And it still seems strange that on the same night as Rangers played Moscow Dynamo in Barcelona, Scotland took on Wales in the Home International Championship at Hampden thus preventing the final going out live to the nation.[6]

However, the national team had age-old problems. Contrary to the myth that Scotland teams of yesteryear were world beaters, they had in fact failed to qualify for the previous three World Cup Finals ('62 ,'66, '70), highlighting the dearth of quality players, particularly strikers, able and willing to pull on the dark blue jersey. Tommy Docherty took over as national team boss from Bobby Brown during season 1971/72 and gave a debut to Arsenal's 'English' goalkeeper Bob Wilson. Also, interesting speculation centred on the possibility that Scotland would cap Ted McDougall, at the time playing for English third division club Bournemouth. *Plus ca change*.[7]

From Rangers' point of view, the new season offered a fresh opportunity to overcome their bitter rivals Celtic. The Ibrox team was in transition (as it turned out, a long transition) and more in hope than expectation, looking to recapture the successful period of the early sixties. And almost naturally, the success of one Old Firm team heaped disproportionate pressure on the other. The Parkhead team, with Jock Stein at the helm, had already won six League titles on the trot, numerous domestic cups and with a European Cup victory behind them, they seemed invincible.

The tormented Ibrox club had in place a relatively new management duo of Willie Waddell and Jock Wallace. Waddell, a journalist and ex-Rangers player had already won a league championship at Kilmarnock, a remarkable feat in itself and had replaced Davie White in December 1969 after the Ibrox club had crashed out of Europe to unknown Polish side Gornik. 'Deedle' began to impose his own brusque style of management which, as was the norm at that time, owed little to the egalitarian ideal.

Wallace had joined Rangers from Hearts in the summer of the 1970/71 season and brought with him a now legendary reputation for the pursuit of fitness.

Both were 'Rangers men', certainly comfortable with the restrictive Ibrox signing policies, and would subsequently gain the respect of the fans. Only Wallace, however, would eventually become loved by the Ibrox faithful with an affection that eluded the manager. Waddell, often cantankerous and infamously prone to bouts of bad temper, remained distant from the rank and file bluenoses whilst Wallace conversely, could have effortlessly reclaimed his seat on the supporters' bus.

And almost to a man, Waddell and Wallace gained the respect of the players. Respect came from the new ideas the manager brought to an Ibrox team traditionally used to playing off the cuff. Although Waddell's football philosophy seems antiquated now, it was almost pioneering at the beginning of the seventies.

Willie Johnston said, 'Waddell was a great believer in watching our opponents and preparing for games. In the early sixties Rangers were tactically naive and it was all down to yourself how you played the game. But Waddell started to change that thinking and for one thing he made sure you knew the strengths of the team you were playing against.'[8]

Alex MacDonald concurred, 'He brought in photographs of the opponents and the long team talks. We took the photos away home with us and there was no question that you knew the guy you were playing against because you had already done your homework on them. But he could be hard work at times. He could have an argument with three different people in the same room at the same time. He told you what he thought but ten seconds later he'd be asking you, Where are you going tonight, anywhere nice? He never carried a grudge and it was something I took into management with me.'[9]

Allied to the manager's new tactical methods was Wallace's introduction of a new fitness regime. 'Big Jock' subsequently became famous, if not infamous, for his tough training sessions and it was certainly a fit Rangers side that looked forward to the new season.

Colin Stein remembered, 'Training was very hard but I enjoyed it. When I left to go to Coventry I couldn't believe it, their training was a dawdle in comparison. Jock always felt that pre-season training was important because that stood you in good stead for the rest of the season. As everyone knows we used to go to the sand dunes at Gullane and at that time I felt as if I could run for ever.'[10]

Alex MacDonald has similar memories, 'The smaller guys would all lift the same weights as the bigger players like John Greig and Peter McCloy. At times wee Tam McLean and

Willie Waddell contemplates his next game plan

me would come out of training shattered. But I used to thoroughly enjoy Gullane, it was an individual training and it was really good for us at the time. Colin Stein and me were fit and Sandy Jardine could also go all day. There was no specialist goalkeeper coach at that time, so big Peter was on the track with the rest of us. He was told he had the lung capacity of a 1500m runner, which shows you the running he was doing at that time for a goalkeeper.'[11]

Ibrox newcomer Tommy McLean had less fond memories of his initial encounters with Wallace: 'In the early part of my career I struggled to adapt to the different training methods which were based on weight training. My own playing weight went up from nine stone four at Kilmarnock to nine stone twelve at Ibrox. With the weights he had me lifting, I felt I was leaving all my strength in the gymnasium and I had to speak to him about it. But to be fair, he was receptive and altered things to suit me.'[12]

In addition to introducing new training methods, Wallace was also big on team spirit, a feature of Rangers' success in Europe that term and in subsequent seasons on the domestic

Assistant in season 1971/72 was the ever popular Jock Wallace, here in the shower in the Nou Camp Stadium in Barcelona with the European Cup Winners Cup

front. Alex MacDonald said, 'There was a noticeable change when big Jock arrived and not just in terms of training. He was good at getting people together. When I first went there were little cliques in the dressing room, not in a nasty sense but different little groups would all go their own way. But Jock made sure we were all together when we went out on pre-season trips or when we were abroad.'[13]

Innovation, changes and new developments continued off the field. Before the season began in earnest Rangers introduced their new magazine, the *Rangers News* which gave the club a unique platform. Interestingly, in Waddell's first column, he criticised the lack of application on the players' part the previous season stating that, 'there was a shortage of dedication in the league programme which let the club down.'

He also made clear his desire to win the league championship, 'This is the vital issue for Rangers in the new season – more than anything we want to win that flag. The fans have stood behind the club in some lean years. They must now be given their reward for that tremendous support.'[14]

The Ibrox club had cause for pre-season optimism. On top of McLean's arrival from Rugby Park, youngsters Derek Johnstone, Alfie Conn and Derek Parlane were pushing for a regular first team spot and a successful summer tour of Sweden was followed by victories at Ibrox against top English sides, Everton and Spurs. Rangers looked 'Ready' but the players weren't kidded, they knew how tough it was going to be. Alex MacDonald recalls, 'We weren't thinking about winning the league, we were only thinking about putting a run together.'[15] Willie Johnston added, 'We were under pressure because Celtic were a very good team and it was going to be hard to displace them.'[16]

The scene was set for another season in Rangers' history. But there was no hint of what was to follow.

Barcelona – here we come!

3

THE JOURNEY BEGINS: RENNES

Alex MacDonald leads Colin Stein, Willlie Henderson and Andy Penman in a song

*Rennes' 'keeper Aubour makes a save
at Ibrox with Stein waiting to pounce*

Barcelona – here we come!

'They said we were a dirty team and that if we had been in the front line in the Second World War, it would have only lasted a week.'
Peter McCloy

Rangers looked forward to season 1971/72 knowing their opponents in the first round of the Cup Winners Cup would be the French side Rennes. It wasn't exactly a frightening prospect. The current standing of French football, in international terms, cannot be higher and the present European and World Champions were undoubtedly **the** international team of the late nineties. However, their club sides have never emulated that success and only two French teams have won major European trophies. Paris St Germain captured the Cup Winners Cup in 1996 and Marseilles, in dubious circumstances, won the 1992/93 Champion's League. [1]

Rennes, from the North West of France, have only ever won two trophies in their 101 year history, both of them French Cup victories, in 1965 and 1971. Their best ever position in the top League was fourth, in 1965, although they beat the eventual Champions Nantes home and away that season.

Rennes supporter Greg Pichet said, 'We are Bretons and are very proud of it. If we go abroad we prefer to say we are Bretons rather than French although it is only a minority who strive for independence. Younger supporters are told that the great team of 1965 are the best in our history alongside the 1971 side. It was the same trainer, Jean Prouff, on both occasions and some of the players were in both cup-winning sides. But there has been a lot of internal politics since Prouff was sacked in 1972. We went down to the second division in 1975/76 and went up and down for the next eighteen years or so. We came up in 1993 and have settled down now.' [2]

The Bretons weren't packed with household names although their star goalkeeper Marcel Aubour had been in the French national team that had played in the 1966 World Cup in England. Experience of European football was all on the Ibrox side. Rennes' tie against Rangers was only their second ever in European competition and indeed their recent 1999 Intertoto Cup campaign notwithstanding, they have never been involved since. [3] It seemed a relatively straightforward tie for Rangers but by the time the two teams faced up to each other, it was a much closer call.

The Ibrox club had a nightmare start to their domestic campaign and had been defeated three times at home by Celtic before they boarded the plane to Brittany. The season opened with a

Captain John Greig exchanges club pendants with his Rennes counterpart

consolation for the stunned Ibrox fans.

Thus, far from going into their European game with confidence, Rangers were in tatters. Before the first leg in France, in a prelude to the modern day newspaper and radio phone-ins, angry and disillusioned Rangers fans offered their own solutions to the early season slump. One supporter reckoned the Ibrox club should yet again re-sign Jim Baxter, whom Waddell had let go shortly after taking over as manager. Another Baxter devotee concurred, 'What have we won since Baxter left? Nothing, and that's the cause of the slide.'[4]

hectic League Cup section format and in a seventeen-day period Rangers played home and away against Celtic, Ayr United and Morton. The opening day 2-0 defeat against Celtic, which was played at Ibrox due to the reconstruction of Celtic Park, was followed a fortnight later by a 3-0 deficit at the same venue by the same team. In between there were three comfortable wins against Ayr (4-0) Morton (2-0) and Ayr (4-0 again). However, a 1-0 win over Morton wasn't enough to prevent the Ibrox side crashing out of the League Cup before the League campaign had started.

If that early set-back meant that Rangers could 'concentrate on the league' then no-one told the players because their start to that competition was even poorer. An opening game 3-2 defeat at Partick Thistle was followed by yet another loss to Celtic at Ibrox, the slimmer margin of 3-2 being scant

Manager Waddell shrugged off the criticism and attempted to put on a brave face claiming, 'It's not as if we're playing badly.'[5] The forthcoming trip to Brittany offered a welcome break from the domestic stress and indeed the Ibrox players and fans were relaxed about the prospect of Rennes.

Sandy Jardine recalls, 'We gave them respect but French football wasn't that great at the time although they had a good team. But the feeling amongst the players was that it was a nice place to visit.'[6] Supporter Billy McMahon, also had little trepidation about the draw and said, 'We only really knew about Rheims, Raymond Kopa and Just Fontaine who had scored a lot of goals in the World Cup and whose record stood for years. We had beaten Monaco years before that but that's really all we knew about French football.'[7]

Across the Channel, Rangers'

Barcelona – here we come!

opponents and the French press looked forward to Rennes' first European tie in six seasons although the pre-match build-up had a slightly unusual tone. The popular French newspaper *Ouest-France* mischievously introduced the religious element onto the agenda (and indeed subsequently continued that theme) claiming that manager Waddell, 'raised in the Protestant traditions of the club', was hurting because his club were declining at the same time as the 'rise of Catholic Celtic'. [8]

The Bretons were second top of the French First Division when the two teams faced up for the first time ensuring that a tie, which was always going to be difficult for the Scots, had an added degree of difficulty. Significantly, Rangers lined up with an unusually rigid 4-4-2 with Stein and Johnston, a combination that was to prove so potent as the campaign went on, spearheading the attack.

Goalkeeper Peter McCloy claims, 'We played a different system in Europe and it seemed to suit us better with the players we had.' [9] Rangers' league form suggested defensive problems and they searched for a disciplined and organised rearguard that would form the foundation for a European run and of course an upturn in league fortunes. Jardine admits, 'We had been losing silly goals, so on the Tuesday night before the game Willie and Jock drilled us for an hour on corners, free kicks, and set pieces. It worked out well for us on the night.' [10]

First Leg Rennes 1 Rangers 1

September 15th 1971

Rennes – Aubour, Cosnard, Cedolin, Chlosta, Cardiet, Garcia (Redon), Keruzore, Terrier, Musjov (Periault), Betta, Lenoir. (scorer – Redon 78 mins)

Rangers – McCloy, Jardine, Mathieson, Greig, McKinnon, Jackson, McLean, MacDonald, Stein, Penman, Johnston. (scorer – Johnston 68 mins)

Although they returned with a good result Rangers by no means entertained the Bretons with a display of scintillating, attacking football. The match was a turgid, stop-start affair which suited Rangers more than their French hosts. It was a night for determination and commitment so unsurprisingly the best Scots' performances came from John Greig and Alex MacDonald, the latter of whom manager Waddell described afterwards as 'outstanding'. [11] The two Rangers midfield men kept close tabs on Rennes playmakers Betta and Keruzore, thus stifling much of the French side's creativity.

Rangers survived an opening assault on their goal with McCloy boosting his defence's confidence with some good handling. A series of corners, nine in all, in the first ten minutes had the Ibrox men pinned back but the Gers' defence obviously remembered their pre-match practice session and defended stoutly. Gradually the Scots found their feet and began to make the occasional break forward. When Colin Stein won a foul just outside the

Rennes penalty area, Andy Penman sent the resultant free-kick wide of the post, laying a marker for the goal threat of the visitors.

The half-time whistle brought a sense of a confidence to the Scots who came out after the break in a more adventurous and aggressive mode. Events took a positive turn for Rangers in the 68th minute when Willie Johnston opened his account for the campaign. A Tommy McLean corner high into the penalty area was missed by the incoming Stein but Johnston was handily placed behind to score from close range.

Johnston, a member of the Rangers side who had lost the 1967 Cup Winners Cup final in Nuremberg said, 'I don't remember the goal, to be honest, but I do remember it was the widest park I had ever played on. It suited me down to the ground, there was plenty of room for me. They weren't a bad team but our talent was that we could score goals away from home.' [12]

Alex MacDonald remembers Johnston's contribution well saying, 'Wee Bud was electric that night. The rest of the players were getting a buzz from it as well, we were trying to get the ball to him so he could go and do his stuff.' [13]

The Ibrox men's lead was short-lived however and it took Rennes only ten minutes to strike back. For once Betta escaped the clutches of MacDonald and his cross from the right was met by substitute Redon who slid in to score at the back post. It was a blow to the Ibrox team who had looked so solid and compact. But nevertheless in the light of their league record it was an acceptable scoreline away from home and it was one that Rangers were to repeat twice more in the campaign.

The Ibrox side flew out of France pleased with their efforts and confident of finishing the tie off in the return match. The French, however, were outraged, almost insulted at how Rangers had set about their task. Their talented midfielder and playmaker Raymond Keruzore complained frustratedly about the treatment he had received from Greig, 'There was nothing I could do, there was a player shadowing me everywhere I went.' [14]

Manager Jean Prouff, who had coached Standard Liege to victory over Rangers almost ten years earlier in the European Cup, was fuming and fired the opening salvo in a war of words saying, 'Rangers did not play football here, what they did had nothing to do with football. They came only to defend. They took the spectacle out of the game and the fans here in Brittany feel cheated.' [15]

Ouest France journalist Roger Glemee, perhaps showing his European naivety, complained that Rangers, 'forgot what the ball was for'. His colleague, Andre Mausson, in similarly righteous mode grumbled, 'The Scots in the most unpleasant of means achieved their goal', before adding the classic French insult, with obvious

Barcelona – here we come!

Stein comes close against Rennes at Ibrox

malice aforethought, that the whole affair, 'had not been very catholic'. [16]

Under-pressure Waddell couldn't have cared less and in his own abrupt manner barked, 'It is not the responsibility of Rangers to please the Rennes fans.' [17] McCloy, who had a fine performance in goal, recalled with a smile, 'We'd heard they had said we were a dirty team and that if we had been in the front line in the Second World War, it would have only lasted a week. That raised a laugh and we took it as a back-handed compliment. The foreigners weren't happy when they got knocked about a bit.' [18]

The *Glasgow Herald's* reaction to the game makes for interesting reading and reveals the different attitude to on-field discipline at that time. Rangers were complimented on their display, 'despite three (players) booked' and it was also noted that Willie Johnston had experienced, 'mixed fortunes because he was booked and scored.'(!) [19] Most modern day players and fans would be glad to take this trade-off. The comment indicates that the booking of a player was more of an issue thirty years ago than in the present day.

The good result did little to kick-start Rangers' league campaign. True, after three league defeats, Rangers won their first points of the season the following Saturday with a 3-0 win over Falkirk but immediately regressed in the next fixture, losing 2-0 at home to an admittedly strong Aberdeen team. The rattled Ibrox club found themselves fifth from bottom of an 18-team league and the vultures began to hover.

Waddell dismissed the crisis calls but the Scottish press were not to be dissuaded and before the return leg Ken Gallacher of the *Daily Record* warned that, 'Alarming gaps must be plugged, otherwise the Ibrox club could be out of Europe.' [20] On a similarly pessimistic note Alastair Gregor of the *Daily Express* advised that, 'Victory is a must if they are to avoid a real crisis at Ibrox.' [21] One assumes that Rangers were only enduring a 'normal' crisis at that point.

The French fourth estate, looking forward to their trip abroad, paid little attention to the on-field plight of their opponents preferring instead to concentrate on their destination. A bleak, 'tenements and shipyards' picture of Glasgow was painted for the 200 Rennes fans making the trip to Scotland and travelling supporters were warned that when Rangers fans, 'were lubricated with whisky, their vocal cords are indestructible'. The intensity of the Old Firm rivalry, always of interest to outsiders, was remarked upon also and it was revealed, with a touching naivety, that Celtic fans had sent letters of encouragement to Rennes coach Jean Prouff. [22]

The French were confident and Prouff, obviously assured of his importance to his employers, arrived in Glasgow claiming somewhat bizarrely, 'The result is not important to us, it is

the way we play and the correct way is by attacking. I will not lose my job if we get beat.' [23] A different era indeed.

The result of course was always of crucial importance to Rangers and the most significant team news for the Ibrox fans was that winger Willie Henderson had been recalled to the starting eleven for the first time that season. Having brought McLean from Kilmarnock, Waddell was unconcerned about the future of Henderson, a situation which ultimately brought about the departure of the wee winger. It was to be an ignominious end to the Ibrox career of a player who had enthralled the Rangers supporters since he himself had taken over from Alex Scott in the early sixties. But Henderson had made a temporary peace and was to play an important part in the Govan side's victory.

Second Leg – Rangers 1 Rennes 0
(Aggregate 2-1)
September 28th 1971
Rangers – McCloy, Jardine, Mathieson, Greig, McKinnon, Jackson, Henderson, Conn, Stein, MacDonald, Johnston. (scorer – MacDonald 38 mins)
Rennes – Aubour, Cosnard, Cardiet, Chlosta, Garcia, Cedolin, Chlosta, Terrier (Musjov), Keruzore (Redon), Betta, Lenoir.

Arguably this game typified the attitude and mentality of early seventies' Scottish football fans. Rangers' early season problems, in part, had been due to the pressure from the terracings to throw caution to the wind from the first whistle. As the Ibrox men steamed forward they would inevitably get caught on the break. Against the French they avoided this costly recklessness – and were criticised by their supporters!

Rangers took control of the game in the early stages and it was clear that as long as they avoided silly mistakes and kept their shape then the visitors would cause few problems. Henderson understandably played like a man with a point to prove and set up Johnston only to see him slam the ball against the keeper Aubour. Moments later the keeper again found himself busy having to dive at Henderson's feet to stop the little winger putting the home side ahead.

However, few teams, no matter how dominant they are in a game, retain concentration for the whole 90 minutes and the French had a real chance to score after some slack Rangers defending. Lenoir, Rennes' top scorer the previous season, had a great opportunity when he found himself in the clear but, as memorably described by the *Glasgow Herald's* Jim Parkinson, '(Lenoir) had all the time in the world to score. But somehow he wanted even longer and the chance was lost.' [24]

Rangers got the important opener through Alex MacDonald in 38 minutes, the midfielder on hand to score after a Willie Johnston shot had been parried by Aubour. It was to become something of a trademark goal for the midfielder

and he recalled, 'It was really all down to me getting in to the box as often as I could. That was my game then and Willie and Jock allowed me to do that.' [25]

The second half was comfortable for Rangers although they passed up several chances to ease the tension on the terraces. The more cautious approach the home side adopted didn't go down well with the Ibrox fans who 'slow hand-clapped and jeered' the team when things weren't going their way. [26] Many of the Rangers players interviewed for this book admitted that the team of '71/'72 were more suited to playing a cautious and disciplined type of game but simply weren't allowed to in Scotland. The Ibrox support, like most of the other fans in Scotland, wanted players attacking for 90 minutes straight from the first whistle. It is an attitude that is still prevalent today although some progress has been made in 'educating' fans to be more patient.

However, on the night, Rangers got away with their reticence to throw everyone forward and, in fact, could have added to their tally. Colin Stein, who had missed a couple of earlier chances, came close when his angled shot came off the cross bar. Then, the impressive Henderson, who could have had several goals on the night, was denied a stonewall penalty in the closing minutes after Rennes defender Casnard sent him flying in the box. But it was of no consequence and a rather unremarkable match ended with

Rangers safely into the next round. Jardine recalled that, 'It was only a one-goal victory at home but it was a good one-goal win. There was no doubt we were the better team.' [27]

The French agreed with the full back's analysis and indeed Prouff was refreshingly magnanimous in defeat saying, 'Rangers played so much better tonight and Henderson and Johnston were the stars.' [28] Keeper Aubour said, 'Henderson was the difference between the Rangers team which played in France and the one we faced tonight.' [29] The French press also accepted the defeat with good grace and reporter Andre Mausson lamented, 'If only Rennes had the attack of (the then superior) Nantes.' [30]

The Scottish reaction to Rangers' victory further highlights the change in expectations of Scottish teams, in the media as well as amongst the fans, in the past thirty years. Nowadays, any Scottish team winning through the first round proper of a European trophy, by hook or by crook, would be deemed as a success but in 1971 mere progress to the second round wasn't considered noteworthy. Winning with some style was required.

Consequently not all the Scottish press were satisfied and in particular Jim Blair of the *Evening Times* was severely critical of the Ibrox men. Under the banner headline, No Poise In Rangers Win, Blair panned Waddell's side saying, 'Tactics are very much part of modern day football but Rangers still indulge in the big kick, the boom-bang-bang business that makes nonsense of all pre-match planning.' [31]

The next night in the European Cup Celtic beat BP 1903 Copenhagen 3-0 in front of 53,000 at Celtic Park (watched by the Rennes party). In the UEFA Cup Aberdeen beat Celta Vigo 1-0 to through 3-0 on aggregate in front of 20,000 at Pittodrie and St Johnstone beat Hamburg 3-0 at Muirton to win 4-2 on aggregate. With Dundee also going through 5-2 on aggregate against Danish side Akademisk, it was the first and only time that five Scottish teams have progressed through to the second round of European competitions.

Back at Ibrox everyone looked forward to the draw and it was Sporting Lisbon who came out of the hat. The Portuguese side were a notch above Rennes and again it was going to be a difficult tie.

Barcelona – here we come!

c h a p t e r

4

SPORTING LISBON

The second leg of the tie with Sporting Lisbon turned out to be a night for the rule book. Here Rangers players wait anxiously in the corridor in the after-match confusion

Rangers directors David Hope, John Lawrence and Matt Taylor
wait at the airport en route to Lisbon. Players Jim Denny and
Peter McCloy are behind. The Rangers party's flight was
delayed and they arrived in Lisbon with little time to spare
before the UEFA deadline

Barcelona – here we come!

'I never knew about the away goals rule, I thought we were out.' Willie Johnston

Rangers seemed determined not to let their positive result against Rennes affect their league performances. On the Saturday after the French were despatched, the Ibrox men's poor domestic form returned and they went down 2-1 away to Hearts. The Govan club had East Fife to thank for keeping them off the bottom of the league and any European success was forgotten as football's old friend 'crisis' made its way once more down the Copland Road.

Despite the cosy relationship between football clubs and the media, the Scottish press couldn't look a gift horse in the mouth. Rangers were there to be shot at and in the *Daily Express*, John Mackenzie savaged the Ibrox team, claiming their display was, 'The most pathetic performance that I can ever remember. This was the most lifeless, the most stereotypical, unimaginative team I can remember in Rangers colours. Rangers and Willie Waddell have reached a crossroads.'[1] And Rangers fans think the modern day media is hard on them!?

Express readers, for the second time that season, were urged to phone in with the solution to Rangers' problems. If modern Ibrox fans, bloated with recent success, are often too quick to complain – and they are – then in early October 1971 those who frequented

the Copland Road slopes had valid cause for complaint. The supporters' grievances were numerous and varied, 'end bigotry and sign a catholic', 'too much emphasis on physical fitness', 'tactics are deplorable', 'non-existent youth policy' and 'over-trained'. The players were castigated and suggestions for possible new signings, always a panacea for fans, were forthcoming in the shape of players such as Drew Jarvie (Airdrie), Donald Ford (Hearts) and Jim Steele (Dundee).[2]

However, in their next game, with Waddell in Portugal checking up on Sporting, Rangers overcame fellow strugglers East Fife 3-1 to alleviate the pressure before hammering Dundee United 5-1 at Tannadice in a performance later described by Sandy Jardine, perhaps in an overcompensatory manner, as 'the best football we've played in five years'.[3] The Portuguese however, had their own scout in Dundee who, employing classic European football psychology, said afterwards, 'If Rangers show first half form like that I'm afraid Sporting Lisbon will not have much interest left in the tournament.'[4]

Interest in the fortunes of Rangers understandably came also from the Portuguese press. The Lisbon newspaper *A Bola* had sent a reporter a week earlier for the Rangers versus East

Fife game and his paper ran the less than complimentary headline, Scottish Football – Everything Runs: the Ball, the Players, the Brain.[5] Commenting on the Dundee United game, *A Bola's* headline screamed, They're A Lot Of Big Horses. The story revealed that the Ibrox men had, 'frightened Dundee Utd to death . . . It seems that the modest form of Rangers ended when they drew Sporting in the Cup Winners Cup.'

Evaluating the Govan men on a man-for-man basis the Portuguese paper said, 'The keeper (Peter McCloy) is very, very tall, has good hands and good reflexes . . . In defence, only Greig stood out – he's more than a defender because he attacks like a grown up, hoofing the ball upfield (for Alex MacDonald's third goal) or going up there himself, and that's how they got the fourth goal . . . Jardine is fulcral to all Rangers attacks, well aided by Fyfe and Penman . . . Henderson is not really fully in form, he dribbles too much and over-complicates things. On the other hand, MacDonald, on the other flank, was a sensation – he has a common name but he's an uncommon player. . . But the great demolition man is Stein.'[6]

The Portuguese were clearly both amused and bemused by Scottish football in general. *A Bola* noted that, 'The Rangers-Celtic rivalry is not what they say – there are no deaths. The BBC and the London newspapers always exaggerate the number of arrests. . . Rangers are intransigent and play only Protestants. A great player who is a Catholic has no place at Ibrox. . . The Rangers crowd whistled Rapid Vienna recently because they have the same colours as Celtic – just like Sporting!'[7]

Rangers may have stopped the domestic rot, whilst at the same time alarming their next European opponents but they were still well short of Championship form and after seven league games they found themselves in ninth position and struggling to stay in contention. Their upcoming Portuguese opponents, conversely, were altogether in better shape. Sporting, traditionally one of Portugal's big two along with Benfica, were currently leading their country's First Division, winning their first six league games, and they arrived in Glasgow with a formidable reputation.

They had won the Cup Winners Cup in 1963/64, beating MTK Budapest 1-0 after a replay. In the early seventies Sporting were the second team in the country after Benfica, whose players made up the bulk of the national team. Domestically, they were successful, winning the League in 1969/70 and they would subsequently win it again in 1973/74. They had won the cup trophy of Portugal in 1970/71, which of course qualified them to subsequently meet Rangers, and they would go on to win it again in 1972/73 and in 1973/74 (therefore completing the Portuguese domestic double that season). Sporting would come third in the league that season behind Benfica and Vitoria de

Setabul and when they arrived in Glasgow they had with them the formidable Hector Yazalde. The Argentinian's nickname was Chirola but ironically, some also called him 'O Abono de Familia' (The Family Subsidy) – for all the goals he scored which won numerous bonuses for his team-mates and their families. This was his first season for the club and he would score 46 goals in the 73/74 season – a domestic record to this day. He was also to be top scorer in 1974/75 with 30 goals. The Govan men had their work cut out to progress through to the next round.

Rangers captain John Greig suffered from several injuries that season but his most bizarre was the one at training just before the visit of Sporting. Jardine recalled, 'We were down training at Largs and Greigy, whilst keeping his eye on a ball, ran into a bench and demolished it. He got up and there was blood everywhere. He got stitches under his chin and played that night.'[8] Greig, now unable to shave, decided to grow a goatee beard and famously vowed not to shave it off until Rangers were out of Europe.

Jardine himself had been successfully converted into a right back and was the only Ibrox player picked a week earlier to play for Scotland against Portugal at Hampden where Sporting had two players on display, Damas and Calo. Benfica supplied eight of the Portuguese team showing where the balance of power in Lisbon lay at that

time. There was another, more tenuous, Ibrox link in that game. Arsenal keeper, one Robert Primrose Wilson, made his debut in a 2-1 victory watched by 58,000 spectators. Wilson's great-uncle Sir John Ure Primrose, former Lord Provost of Glasgow, was the President of the Ibrox club at the beginning of the century and had formally opened Hampden in 1903. The *Daily Record* suggested that there would be a 'special Rangers cheer' for the keeper.[9] How times have changed! [10]

First Leg
Rangers 3 Sporting Lisbon 2
20th October 1971
Rangers – McCloy, Greig, Mathieson, Jardine, McKinnon, Smith, Henderson, Penman (Conn), Stein, Fyfe, MacDonald. (scorers – Stein 9, 19, Henderson 28)
Sporting Lisbon – Damas, Laranjiero (Lourenco), Hilario, Goncalves (Gomes), Calo, Jose Carlos, Chico, Nelson, Yazalde, Vagner, Dinis. (scorers – Chico 70, Gomes 86)

Rangers' first half performance should have made the return leg a formality as they raced into a three goal lead. Disorientated by a swirling wind, the Portuguese failed to cope with the early Ibrox onslaught, especially their keeper Damas who was at fault for the first two goals. The first counter came after only nine minutes when Corbor fouled Stein, and from the Penman free-kick, it was Stein himself who headed home with Damas floundering in mid-air.

The sight of Stein being clattered from behind was a familiar feature of the campaign but he claimed, 'Foreign players weren't as physical as the home grown players. They were more clever, they would jockey you into less dangerous positions. The average Scottish player would dive in and sell himself. But don't get me wrong, you don't usually get small centre-halfs and there was some big guys who could give you a whack when they wanted.' [11]

Stein survived the rough treatment but the free kick was more or less Andy Penman's last contribution to the game and indeed the campaign as he limped off shortly afterwards to be replaced by young Alfie Conn. Rangers had total control of proceedings with Sporting chasing shadows. The second goal came only ten minutes later as a result of yet another set piece, this time after Henderson was impeded by Nelson. Dave Smith crossed into the centre and again Stein scored what he described as 'a thumper – I met the cross with my head and the connection was just right.' [12]

The third goal came from Willie Henderson. The little winger worked a free kick with substitute Conn and fired a tremendous shot from the corner of the penalty area which gave the hapless Damas no chance. The goal should have signalled the end of the tie and keeper McCloy certainly thought so. He recalled, 'When we turned round at half time we had the wind at our backs.

I thought we'd go on and score more goals because for some reason foreign teams didn't travel too well.' [13] The big Ibrox keeper couldn't have been more wrong.

Despite being urged on by the crowd, the Ibrox men couldn't reproduce their first half form and the visitors rallied. Rangers were caught in a tactical no-man's land, not quite sure how to tackle a game they had all but sewn up. Of course, simply defending their comfortable lead wasn't one of the options available and in the end they paid the price for their hesitancy. In the 70th minute Yazalde, who had been kept relatively quiet, fired in a shot which was parried by McCloy. The Brazilian Chico, looking suspiciously offside, lobbed the keeper and in one brief moment the pendulum swung back towards Sporting.

The visitors now sensed they could rescue the game. Rangers were on the ropes in the latter stages but looked to have held on until the now familiar late European goal was conceded. With only four minutes to go Dinis, whose 'long black legs' were remarked upon in the next morning's newspapers(!), [14] was involved in a move which ultimately saw substitute Pedro Gomez notch the visitors' second goal. The silence inside the ground was deafening as the fans realised the tie was far from the formality the first half hour had promised.

As the disappointed Rangers supporters streamed out of Ibrox however, they could not have foreseen the drama which was to unfold in the return leg.

Both managers, unsurprisingly, had differing views of the game. Waddell was in his usual bullish mood when he said, 'We're in front and they still have to catch us.' A relieved Sporting boss Fernando Vaz said, 'Rangers were a brilliant team in the first half but I am happy with those two goals. Now the tie is in the balance.' [15]

The press, likewise, were diverse in their interpretation and an intriguing literary contrast was revealed. John Mackenzie said, 'The performance of last night's defence in the last half hour leaves me with no confidence that they can stand firm in Lisbon.' [16] Raymond Jacobs in the *Glasgow Herald* said, somewhat clumsily, that 'Rangers' hopes of survival dwindled to the dimensions of a hairline.' [17] Ken Gallacher claimed the first half was, 'just about the finest attacking performance in Europe – last 20 minutes must have been just about most depressing', before going on to say, 'at the moment it looks as if the tie has been lost in the second half fade-out at Ibrox.' [18]

The Portuguese press saw the game and Rangers' performance in a different light. *A Bola* claimed, 'The Scottish goals all came from free kicks that were more than dubious. . . The Scots overindulge in provocations and commit foul after foul. They're hard and, more than hard, they're violent.'

Colin Stein watches as Henderson (out of picture) fires Rangers into a three goal lead at Ibrox

However, there was clear respect for some of the Rangers players and underneath a headline proclaiming, A Hurricane Named Stein, it said, 'Colin Stein was a symbol of the hurricane football played out by Rangers in the first half. . . This young player was a paradigm of the football seen in these beautiful and rainy parts. . . Sandy Jardine was an artist in the art of playing football, full of style and suppleness, a player with talent and class. . . the magnificent Alfie Conn, with a motor that never looked like going out of tune.' [19]

The *Jornal do Sporting's* headline, In Glasgow, A Defeat That's A Victory! was followed by the claim that, 'Everything was against The Lions – the crazy support, the unfavourable weather (more for Sporting) and the value of Rangers – a great team, athletic. . . a fearsome adversary.' Then, getting carried away somewhat, it continued, 'Sporting imposed a frenetic rhythm on the game in the second half: the vibration of the Lions' game spread out like high tension current. The serenity of the nearby Loch Lomond must have been disturbed by this unstoppable, irresistible vibration.'[20]

The Sporting players were similarly respectful and Portuguese internationalist Calo said, with reference to the recent international clash between the two countries, 'I think Rangers' attack is more dangerous than Scotland's. Also, Rangers are more of a team.' The influential Yazalde reiterated a theme of Rangers' campaign when he exclaimed, 'Their defenders are fearsome!'[21] But despite the subversive noises there was no doubt that Sporting fancied their chances of progressing though to the next round.

Rangers fans would have paid scant attention to the small column which appeared at the bottom of the next day's *Glasgow Herald*. It announced that Nottingham Forest had signed a young Irishman from Distillery for a fee of £15,000 with £6000 more to follow when he made six first team appearances and a further £6000 when he made six international appearances. His name was Martin O'Neil.[22]

Rangers had barely time to catch their breath before it was back to league business the following Saturday against Motherwell. Almost bizarrely, to a stranger if not a native, the biggest boost to the Ibrox team came from another game being played on the south side of Glasgow – the Scottish League Cup Final between Partick Thistle and Celtic. It was the Jags' finest hour as they caused a major upset by beating the Parkhead men 4-1.

Urban myths survive of Rangers fans, on hearing the 4-0 half-time score for Thistle, leaving Ibrox in taxis to get over to Hampden to gloat at their rivals' misfortune. Leaving aside the improbability of that happening on any significant scale, the crowd and the teams at Ibrox that day were certainly aware of the shock half-time scoreline at the national stadium. The tannoy announcer relayed the news from Hampden which seemed to boost the home side who, struggling throughout the first half, were lambasted by their fans who booed them off at half time. The second half saw an improvement in the Ibrox men's performance and in the end they ran out easy 4-0 winners. However, Motherwell winger Kirky Lawson was in no doubt about the inspirational powers of the Celtic defeat had had on the Ibrox players saying, 'I'm certain that this acted as a terrific spur to Rangers. Up until then we had just as much of the game.'[23] Not that the Ibrox game made much of an impression elsewhere. The *Glasgow Herald* felt it didn't need to bother with proceedings at Ibrox, carrying match reports of only the League Cup final and the Morton v Aberdeen clash at Cappielow.[24]

The following Saturday Rangers were again at home, this time to Kilmarnock in what was a typical Scottish First Division fixture. Rangers fans could turn up and pay 60p to get into the stand, 40p for the enclosure, 30p for the ground and boys and OAPs 15p. The talking point was the dismissal of Sandy Jardine with the score at 1-1 but a double from Alex MacDonald gave the ten men the two points. Despite the upturn in league fortunes, Rangers remained seven points behind leaders Celtic and even that early in the season it was clear that the Ibrox men's league chances were slim. However, with regards to the return leg in Portugal, Waddell and his players were boosted by the fact the Sporting had lost 2-1 to Belevese.

By all accounts the trip to Lisbon for the team was a nightmare. Due to delays the Rangers party arrived in the Portuguese capital the day before the game, barely three hours before the UEFA deadline. In those days football teams usually had to use the same scheduled flights as the general public when flying abroad and it sometimes involved all the hassle which most holiday makers and travellers have experienced over the years. An air traffic controllers' strike at Glasgow had resulted in the Ibrox party landing in London too late to catch their plane to Lisbon. There ensued an overnight stay in the capital before flying out in the morning. There were rumours that the players even had to carry their own bags at one point! [25] But Waddell tried to play this down by saying, 'The problem is keeping the players occupied. They are starting a game at a time when players are normally

finishing it. They are playing better now, with a string of good results behind us.' [26]

Second Leg – Sporting 4 Rangers 3 (aet)
(Aggregate: Sporting Lisbon 6 Rangers 6) Rangers go through on away goals rule
3rd November, 1971
Sporting Lisbon – Dames, Gomes, Hilario, Tome, Talo, Laranjiero, Vagner, Lourenco, Yazalde, Perez, Dinis (Marinho). (scorers – Yazalde 26, Tome 37, Gomes 83, Perez 114)
Rangers – McCloy, Greig, Mathieson, Jardine, McKinnon (Smith), Jackson, Henderson, Conn, Stein, Johnston (McLean), MacDonald. (scorers – Stein 27, 46, Henderson 100)

The tie became infamous for the Dutch referee Laurens Van Raven's ignorance of the away goals rule which resulted in a penalty shoot-out charade. The referee was no stranger to Scottish football. He had been in charge in 1967 when Rangers beat Zaragoza at Ibrox and in the 1968 Scotland v England clash which ended in a 1-1 draw. But that night in Lisbon Van Raven was, apparently, a stranger to the rules.

The pre-match atmosphere was wonderfully depicted by the Portuguese *Chronicle* newspaper. 'Shortly before kick-off, the Estadio de Alvalade was physically and spiritually full. The stands were crammed, spirits brimming over with faith. Hope, almost certainty,

Second Leg - Sporting 4 Rangers 3 (aet) (Aggregate: Sporting Lisbon 6 Rangers 6) Rangers go through on away goals rule

of recovery was in the air, in everyone's souls.' [27]

The home side, spurred on by their fanatical supporters, took the lead in the 25th minute through Yazalde although the finger of blame pointed to McCloy. The keeper admitted, 'They scored with a long range free-kick which I spilled. Their guy was on top of me like a flash and knocked it into the net. So I had to listen to the boys giving me stick afterwards. But I didn't have a lot of European experience at that time and the lighter ball caught me out a bit at times. If you took your eye off it for a fraction of a second, you were in trouble.' [28]

In present day European football, that goal would have perhaps heralded a tactical change from the home team knowing that they were through on away goals. Perhaps it might have done if Colin Stein, rampaging through the Portuguese defence, hadn't equalised barely two minutes later. In 37 minutes Sporting's lead was restored through Tome and once again the home side had the away goals advantage going into the break.

We'll never know how the Portuguese would have approached the second period because Stein waited only a minute before he equalised on the night for the second time and the balance of the tie was back on the blue side. Stein recalls, 'I had fancied us to score there. They were a good football-ing team and they played open football. They didn't try and shut up shop which they could have done once they got the first goal. But what stood out for me over there was that it was a packed house and they had a big row of drummers along the side making this constant noise throughout the game.' [29]

Sporting, now with little option left, went all out for the goal which would take the game into extra-time. Their cause seemed to be helped when the Rangers defence was weakened after defender Ronnie McKinnon broke his leg in a tackle. Alex MacDonald recalls, 'I remember big Ronnie lying on the ground. We were all buzzing about, playing away and he was just sitting there and we're saying to him, Come on, get up. There was no agony or rolling about from him, he was just sitting there with his hand up as if to say, Excuse me, I've broken my leg, can you get me an ambulance!' [30]

But the Ibrox men were hardly weakened as it was the immaculate Dave Smith, at the peak of his form, who came on as substitute. McKinnon was stretchered off with an injury which, sadly, effectively ended his Rangers career.

Nevertheless, Sporting made it 3-2 only six minutes from the end through Gomes and it was the home side who now held the trump card having an extra 30 minutes in front of their frenzied support in which to win the tie. But Rangers refused to buckle and equalised for the third time on the night, ten minutes into extra time through Henderson. Circumstances had

Barcelona – here we come!

changed again. Another goal for Sporting would tie the game overall but Rangers would have scored more away from home.

But there were no thoughts of penalties or away goals. Play raged on from end to end and Sporting indeed scored the goal which ultimately caused all the confusion. Just before the extra time interval, Perez scored with a penalty and when the final whistle went with the score 4-3 for Sporting and 6-6 on aggregate, the referee lined the teams up for penalties.

Amongst the Rangers players, confusion reigned. Colin Stein says, 'I was adamant that we were through and I said so to big Peter but what can you do when the ref tells you take penalties?[31]

Peter McCloy recalls, 'I thought maybe Steiny was right but I thought

we'll just have to get on with it.'[32]

Willie Johnston however, says, 'I never knew about the away goals rule, I thought we were out.'[33] Sandy Jardine concurs saying, 'We didn't think about it, as far as I was concerned it was penalties. Just before I took my penalty Willie Johnston was sitting down on the pitch with one of their players talking about nice wine and restaurants!'[34]

It was just as well the referee had made a mistake because the penalties were a disaster for Rangers who took the spirit of, 'all-for-one and one-for-all' to absurd heights. The Scots missed their first four and Dave Smith in particular seemed particularly keen not to score, missing at a second opportunity after the referee had ordered a re-take. Skipper John Greig didn't even get to take the fifth penalty.

Colin Stein gives Sporting keeper Damas no chance with a powerful header

The Rangers players sloped back to the dressing room convinced they were out of the competition. Sandy Jardine said, 'We were all sitting there with our heads in hands as their goalkeeper Damas, ironically the keeper who was so poor at Ibrox, was chaired around the pitch. We all sat there feeling sorry for ourselves.' [35]

The ecstatic Portuguese fans left the stadium under the impression that their heroes were through to the next round. Many Rangers fans understandably thought their team was out.

John Miller listened to the game on the radio and recalled, 'I went to my bed on a downer thinking they were out and it wasn't until the next morning that I heard they were reinstated.' [36] Jack Bain was at work as the game was played and remembers, 'I was nightshift at the time and all the guys were saying Rangers were out. But I was arguing with them all, saying they were wrong. They didn't think so but later it came over the radio and I was right, Rangers were through.' [37]

The popular myth is that reporter John Fairgrieve's intervention somehow rescued the tie for Rangers by highlighting the rules to Waddell who then went looking for the UEFA delegate to protest. In fact, the UEFA delegate, Andres Ramirez, was fully aware of the referee's mistake. In the Portuguese protest to UEFA the following morning it was acknowledged that Ramirez tried to get down to the pitch side to stop the referee beginning the penalty shoot-out but by the time he arrived Damas had already saved the first penalty. The delegate probably correctly ruled against intervening at that stage. However, given the UEFA penchant for strange decisions it was perhaps best that Waddell flagged up the problem before Rangers had left the stadium. [38]

After the game, Ramirez, gathered together the directors of both clubs, the referee and linesmen and told them that he was going to send a telegram to UEFA reporting that the ref Van Ravens had wrongly interpreted the rules. The Portuguese were understandably fuming. Sporting's president, Guilherme Medeiros, also sent a telegram, claiming initially that the referee's decision should be final since he was sovereign on the field of play. In the telegram, he suggested that two directors fly to Berne to 'defend the prestige of football and sporting ethics and to avoid serious moral and material damage to the club.'

However, by telephone, a UEFA spokesman said there was no need to send anyone because the decision had already been taken: the victory would be attributed to Rangers. On the following Monday, yet another telegram was sent from Sporting to UEFA headquarters but to no avail. [39]

Portuguese journalist Alfredo Farinha of *The Chronicle* said in the aftermath, 'This was another game that will be talked about for many years to come. The narrative of this extraordinary footballing event, in which suspense and drama mixed intermittently with joy and despair, will be handed down from fathers to sons, especially among the Sporting fans who were present.' [40]

The Portuguese were dumbstruck at the outcome but there was praise for the Scots visitors. 'When Rangers had possession, the ball seemed to automatically obey the movements that everybody imposed on it, whether in triangles or long balls. Unlike the style that always characterises the football of the Scottish school, this Rangers team played so openly that its style seemed more like that of English teams, especially coming out of defence, than that of Scottish teams.' Hilario, the Sporting captain said, 'As we expected, Rangers' forwards caused us lots of problems. Stein in particular was sensational.' [41]

But Peter McCloy came in for some harsh criticism, 'However, this magnificent team does not have a goalkeeper of the same level as his team-mates . . . But as the team has a magnificent set of players, from the right back to the left winger; the class of Greig, a defender of extraordinary class, whether tackling or clearing, or putting the ball up front; the magnificent power of Jardine, who was always in evidence in midfield, (both intercepting and laying the ball off); Henderson and Stein up front, good ball-winners and both with a great shot; the lack of class of the goalkeeper can be disguised, as it was last night.' [42] McCloy's team mates had dug the goalkeeper out of a hole that night but

the big keeper would repay the debt in full later in the tournament.

In the following days, however, the Portuguese turned their wrath on UEFA. A front page editorial in the *Jornal do Sporting* cried for Justice! with the front page banner headline screaming, Victory to Sporting or Repetition of the Game. [43] A week later the same newspaper suggested somewhat desperately that Sporting's appeal against the result was rejected because they had not translated it into one of the three official languages of UEFA (French, English, German). [44]

Ultimately, the Lisbon side had to accept the decision and went on to fight another day. Thirty years later, keeper Damas, the Sporting 'hero' on that dramatic night in Lisbon recalled, 'Rangers had a great team, typical of British football. Portuguese teams had not adapted to the British style. The Rangers players were fast, physically strong and good in the air and caused us a lot of difficulties. I don't remember the names of any of the players, but there was a forward, small and fast, very dangerous. But both games were very even. The game in Glasgow was very intense. The stadium was full and the support for the team was fantastic – there was so much noise. It put us off a little. The second game was a high point in my career, on a personal level. An historic game for me and one I remember well, even after so many years. After all, I saved three penalties! The ref ordered penalties to be taken, but the rules had been changed that year, so 1-1 in extra time gave the game to Rangers. We only knew about the problem when the UEFA delegate came to the changing room. Imagine the euphoria and then the disappointment. Yes, there were tears. If we had been a Real or an AC Milan, an appeal would have changed the result.' [45]

Rangers were not the only Scottish success in that European week. In the European Cup Celtic's 3-1 victory over Sliema Wanderers of Malta allowed the Parkhead men to coast through 7-1 on aggregate. In the UEFA Cup Dundee fought back to beat Cologne 4-2 to win 5-4 on aggregate in what was arguably the Tayside club's finest hour in Europe. Vasas of Hungary beat St Johnstone 1-0 but the Perth men won 2-1 on aggregate. Scotland's only second round European victors were Aberdeen who lost out 3-1 to Juventus over two legs.

Fixtures were coming thick and fast and on the following Saturday, Stein was again in fine form as Rangers beat St Johnstone 4-1 in a bad tempered game which saw Willie Waddell and Jock Wallace on the pitch at one point trying to restore order amongst the brawling players. There was no rest for Sandy Jardine, who was Rangers' only representative the following Wednesday when Scotland beat Belgium 1-0 at Pittodrie, a result which landed Tommy

Docherty the manager's job on a full time basis.

It was the kind of relentless schedule that would take its toll on the Rangers defender. He recalled, 'That season I played more than 70 games because I had also been playing in the under-21s, and had a couple of inter-league games. After Barcelona, Scotland were going on a tour of South America. I pulled out of the squad because I had played so much football that season. I was never injured and never missed a game so I was knackered. I phoned Tommy Docherty who was the manager and told him I needed a rest. He said, No problem I understand, it doesn't matter, – but I never got picked under his reign again! But he didn't last long and I got back in.' [46]

The Dundee game at Ibrox the following Saturday brought Rangers down to earth with a bump. It was yet another disappointing league display, one of several that season that had no real explanation. In a first half collapse, they lost three goals and although it was pulled back to 2-3, the points, along with the faint Championship hopes vanished. The League was over for Rangers in November. In European terms Rangers now had a lengthy four month wait until the next round which was scheduled for March of the new year. During that lengthy interlude the Ibrox men were to experience some mixed fortunes on the domestic scene.

       Barcelona – here we come!

5

T O R I N O

*Rangers players take in some shopping
and some silly walks in Italy before
the game*

*Rangers' feared striker Colin Stein
looks quite at home in Turin*

Barcelona – here we come!

'Rangers came here and played the Italian game.'
Gustavo Giagnoni, Torino coach

Rangers defeat against Dundee concentrated a few minds and sparked off a run of seven consecutive league wins. Away wins at Morton (2-1) and Ayr United (2-1) completed the rest of the November card and the next month saw Clyde beaten 1-0 at home, Dunfermline beaten 2-0 at East End Park, Airdrie 3-0 at Ibrox and on Christmas day at Easter Road, Colin Stein's last gasp winner gave the travelling support a chance to practise their pitch invasions!

Rangers brought in the New Year beating Partick Thistle 2-1 and then faced up to Celtic two days later in the usual frantic derby fixture. The Ibrox club were playing only for pride but once again the Parkhead men came out on top 2-1 courtesy of a late Jim Brogan winner. The defeat not only ended all pretence of the Rangers' championship hopes, it signalled Celtic, as a club, pulling still further away from their traditional enemy. Jock Stein's men weren't just en route to a domestic record, they too were in the quarter-finals of a European tournament, the superior Champions Cup.[1] This was a competition in which they had reached the final twice before and a trophy they had actually lifted within very recent memory. In January 1972, the Cup-Winners Cup wasn't even a real chance

for Rangers to outshine Celtic – it was the least they could do to keep in touching distance of the Parkhead men.

The January draw for the quarter-finals of the Cup Winners Cup offered some much needed excitement for those of an Ibrox persuasion. Although the Rangers players and fans probably felt their team could cope with anything after the rollercoaster tie with Sporting Lisbon, they would nevertheless have shown an interest in the other seven teams heading for the hat in Zurich: Bayern Munich of West Germany, containing the talents of Golden Boot winner Gerd Muller and *der Kaiser* himself, Franz Beckenbauer, were the team everyone hoped to avoid. Torino, were as daunting an opponent as any Italian team of the day, especially as they were challenging for the Serie A title at the time. Steau Bucharest of Rumania, Red Star Belgrade of Yugoslavia and Dynamo Berlin of East Germany represented the mysterious, always dangerous threat of Eastern Bloc opposition.[2]

While Moscow Dynamo completed the large last eight contingent from behind the Iron Curtain, they were slightly less of a mystery to Rangers fans.[3] Atvidabergs of Sweden would normally have been regarded as the weakest team left in the competition, except for one small matter – in the second round they'd knocked out holders Chelsea. [4] In the event it was Torino who were paired with the Ibrox men – a task which was daunting but not insurmountable.

But there were three months to go before the teams met and in the meantime Rangers sought, with some success, to find some domestic consistency. After the defeat at Parkhead the Ibrox men embarked on another unbeaten League run which lasted all through January and right up to a mid-February defeat at Motherwell. The rest of January saw a 3-1 home win over Falkirk, a goal-less draw at Pittodrie, a tremendous 6-0 thrashing of Hearts at Ibrox, and a slim 1-0 victory at East Fife's Bayview.

The Ibrox men began February with a 2-2 Scottish Cup draw against Falkirk at Brockville before winning the replay 2-0. League business was next and a 1-0 win against Dundee United at Ibrox was followed by the 2-0 defeat at Motherwell. The Ibrox men bounced back with a 4-1 Scottish Cup win over St Mirren at Love Street.

It was therefore a worry for Rangers to be drawn away to Motherwell in the only national competition they could still win, although they hadn't managed to lift the Scottish Cup since 1966. Rangers were due to return to Fir Park on Scottish Cup duty on the 18th of March. Four days later they'd play the second leg of the Torino tie – it was quite conceivable that Rangers' season could be over before April.

Added into this pessimistic mix was the fact that, in three previous attempts, Rangers had never beaten an Italian side in European competition. In the first round proper of the 1957/58 European Cup, AC Milan came to Ibrox and decimated the home side by four goals to one before tying things up with a 2-0 win in Italy. In 1960/61, Fiorentina provided the opposition in the first final of the Cup Winners Cup and won both at Ibrox, 2-0, and in Florence, 2-1. The quarter-final of the 1964/65 Champions Cup was, however, both the most recent encounter with Italian opposition and the nearest Rangers had come to triumphing as Inter Milan lost 1-0 at Ibrox after a 3-1 win in the San Siro. Most Ibrox regulars still felt that Jim Baxter's leg-break against Rapid Vienna in the previous round had cost Rangers a place in the semi-final that year. . . possibly even the final. Seven seasons later, and in another quarter-final, would Torino prove equally frustrating?

Turin and Milan are, of course, the true power-bases of Italian soccer. Rome occasionally chips in with a Lazio or Roma championship victory just as Edinburgh once did in Scotland with Hearts and Hibs but the northern industrial heartland of Italy provides the consistent domination of Serie A and *lo Scudetto* has gone to Turin more often than any other Italian city. Nowadays it's Juventus who, while occasionally the rulers of World and

European football, are certainly the most famous team in Italy and easily the dominant club in Turin.

However, their neighbours Torino were once the greatest team the country had ever seen and while today the *granata* ('The Pomegranates' – after their beautiful burgundy coloured jerseys) are a typical 'yo-yo' side, constantly engaging in promotion from Serie B and relegation from Serie A, in the early seventies they were a force to be reckoned with.

Most Scottish football fans of the day knew the name Torino for two main reasons. Firstly, during the early sixties they were a famous importer of Scottish and English talent – men such as Gerry Hitchens, Hibs' striking legend Joe Baker and the all-time greatest Scottish international goalscorer, Denis Law, had made the Turin club a familiar name in British households long before Channel 4 and James Richardson's *Gazzetta Football Italia* hit our TV screens.

Secondly – the sad story that is known throughout the footballing world – the greatest Torino side of all, perhaps the best Italian club side there ever was, the team now known simply as *Il Grande Torino*, was tragically taken from their supporters in a way which perhaps only the fans of Manchester United's Busby Babes could ever really understand. The word 'Superga' was once known only as the name of a 2,200 ft peak on the outskirts of Turin. Ever since 4th May 1949,

however, when the plane carrying Torino Calcio back from their friendly against Benfica of Portugal collided with the hillside, killing everyone on board, it has become synonymous with the greatest tragedy ever to befall an Italian football team. At that moment it was the greatest peacetime tragedy to befall any football team. The death of an entire planeload of young men is calamitous enough for its own sake but this particular group of men were on course for their fifth successive Italian championship – a record which would equal that set in the thirties by their great rivals, Juventus.

In the days following this tragedy, the Torino youth side completed the club's remaining league fixtures and, with their opponents in their last few games agreeing also to field their youth sides as a mark of respect, Torino duly won their fifth successive *Scudetto*. However, unlike Manchester United, the Italians did not rebuild a side that could repeat the glories of their lost greats.

Torino, when they were drawn to meet Rangers in the 1971/72 quarter-final, were a club still haunted by their tragedy of 23 years earlier. Unlike Munich '58, there were no survivors of Superga, the entire first-team squad had been killed and Torino Calcio had to re-build from scratch. It had been an unbelievably difficult task and, as detailed in Alexandra Manna and Mike Gibbs' *The Day Italian Football Died, Torino and the tragedy of Superga*, far from being a healing process for the fans, piled further pain on the *granata*. Gradually slipping down the league, Torino were relegated from Serie A ten years after Superga and, due to financial constrictions, even had to move out of their beautifully compact, memory-laden and much-loved home. The departure from the Filadelfia ground was made all the more intolerably painful because it meant moving into the Stadio Comunale to share with. . . Juventus!

A quick return to Serie A and the spate of foreign signings in the early sixties lifted spirits but further tragedy struck when their mercurial forward Gigi Meroni was hit by a car and killed in October 1968. Meroni shared the same name as the pilot of the ill-fated Superga plane and this merely heightened the sense that Torino were a club plagued by unbelievable catastrophe. The only thing which could ever remove this conviction was a return of the *Scudetto* or, perhaps, European glory.

Rangers fans who lived through the nine-in-a-row years of Graeme Souness and Walter Smith's reigns can appreciate the passion with which fans will fete a group of players who, wearing their club's colours, equal a record set by their most bitter rivals. However, Rangers teams of 88/89 to 96/97 had only one brief flicker on the European stage – when they were a goal away from the 1993 Champions League final. *Il Grande Torino* were not just a domestic but a continental and international phenomenon. They frequently supplied more than half the Italian national team of the forties and in May 1947 they famously supplied ten players and all the goals in Italy's 3-2 win over Hungary. [5]

In March 1972, Torino still had a real chance of lifting the *Scudetto*, an achievement which would have helped alleviate the pain of previous tragedies. On their third manager in as many seasons, they were challenging strongly for the Serie A title and to add to the pressure and excitement, they were locking horns in the championship battle with their sworn enemies, Juventus. In the post-Superga rebuilding years Juventus had collected a further six Serie A titles to pull away from Torino. However, neither Turin side had, at this stage, made a real impact on the European club competitions. Juve had reached finals, the 1965 and 1971 Fairs Cups, and they managed to lose both. Thirteen years later Juventus would become the first team to win all three of the major European trophies but in 1972, Glasgow had a far greater European pedigree than Turin.

To make matters even more interesting, with both Rangers and Celtic due to play their European quarter-final second legs in the same city on the same night, Juventus and Torino were both due to play their first legs on consecutive nights. . . in the same stadium! Juve were not only competing with Torino on the domestic front they were also busily trying to out-do them in that season's European tournaments, in much the same way as the Old Firm. Rangers would play against Torino in the Stadio Comunale on Wednesday 8th March, the night after *La Vecchia Signora* hosted Wolverhampton Wanderers on the same pitch in the UEFA cup quarter-final. The fact of two Italian sides competing against two British sides in the space of 24 hours was to have more than a coincidental bearing on the Rangers game.

Torino, eighth in the league the previous season, had won the Italian Cup against AC Milan in Genoa after a 0-0 draw and penalty shoot-out. The score-line and the game which produced it were typical of the constricting, deeply-defensive *catenaccio* style of play favoured by Italian sides of the day and Rangers knew goals would be hard to come by. [6] The *granata* had changed their manager since winning the Italian Cup. Charismatic President and self-made businessman Lucio Orfeo Pianelli appointed former Mantova boss Gustavo Giagnoni [7] and the improvement had been immediate as Torino headed to the top of the league after four games and subsequently contested the title with Juventus and Milan for the rest of the season.

Without the big name stars of previous seasons Torino were nevertheless becoming experts at squeezing one goal victories out of matches which had draw written all over them. Former Napoli midfielder,

Claudio Sala, was their best known player and while Paolo Pulici had failed to impress in any of his two previous campaigns – going the whole of 1969/70 season without scoring! – he was on the verge of becoming a legendary figure in the eyes of the Torino fans. In 1971/72 he and Sala were beginning to find the form that by 75/76 would bring the Serie A title back to the burgundy half of Turin. [8] This was a great Italian club side in the making.

Rangers, if anticipating a low-scoring encounter, couldn't take much comfort from the Sporting Lisbon tie. After all they had lost six goals over the two legs. Waddell's men would have to tighten up at the back to an almost unrecognisable extent and they'd find scoring goals immensely more difficult. And there were other obstacles to overcome. In the days where most club sides throughout Europe were populated entirely by players from their own country, national stereotypes and characteristics abounded. In the eyes of British fans, Italian sides liked to moan, commit sneaky fouls, intimidate the referee and, basically, cheat and some Rangers fans had less than fond memories of the Fiorentina game at Ibrox in 1961. [9]

However, there were league games to worry about before the Italians came calling. On 4th March, Rangers beat Kilmarnock 2-1 at Rugby Park which left Willie Waddell's men in third place, nine points behind leaders Celtic although the Govan team had played a game less. Second placed Aberdeen, however, had gone down 2-0 at Firhill and their manager Jimmy Bonthrone had consequently declared the league race over. The Italians were keeping tabs on their upcoming Glasgow opponents and in the Monday's *Daily Record* the Torino manager Signor Giagnoni, who'd travelled over to watch the game in Ayrshire, said, '(Dave) Smith is very, very good – so artistic' whilst 'Greig supplies the strength and power' which his star player Sala would find to his cost. [10] Alongside Giagnoni's remarks appeared Tony Queen the bookmakers' odds on the forthcoming game quoting both the Turin and the Govan sides as 4/5 against qualifying for the semi-finals of the Cup Winners Cup.

One famous Glasgow punter, who could have actually affected the outcome, was looking unlikely to feature in the contest. The *Glasgow Herald* announced, 'Rangers have circularised Scottish and English clubs informing them that Willie Henderson, their former international outside right is available for transfer.' [11] The Dunfermline match, almost three months previously, had been Henderson's last for the first team and in January he'd announced his wish never to play for the club again. It seemed as though a famous Ibrox career was coming to a sad end.

But Henderson's imminent departure was not as significant as it could have been. Tommy McLean had the right wing berth more than adequately covered (which was probably why Henderson knew he had to leave) but Waddell's more immediate problem was the fitness of Derek Johnstone, whose importance had increased since McKinnon's leg break. Pundits were beginning to guess how Rangers would play in Italy and the increased need to defend, coupled with the huge gap still felt after McKinnon's injury in Lisbon, demanded Johnstone play in defence rather than in his equally suited centre-forward slot. A thigh injury sustained in a practice match the previous week saw the 18-year old miss the Kilmarnock game and club physio Tom Craig set to work on the troublesome muscle.

Gerhard 'Gerry' Neef, Rangers' German reserve goalkeeper had sustained an ankle injury in the second string's match versus Killie reserves and he, like Johnstone, was undergoing intense physiotherapy when he was announced as part of the 17-strong party to travel to Italy. With Peter McCloy in full fitness this wasn't too great a worry but Waddell, always the perfectionist, drafted in the third-choice keeper Bobby Watson. The full complement of players read: McCloy, Jardine, Mathieson, Greig, Jackson, Smith, McLean, Conn, Stein, A MacDonald, W Johnston, Fyfe, D Johnstone, Neef, Denny, Miller, I MacDonald, Watson.

The Ibrox party were based in the world famous wine-producing town of Asti, some thirty miles outside Turin.

Barcelona – here we come!

The tranquil location, with a population of around 60,000 was far enough from the stadium to allow the players to relax but close enough to circumvent the chance of any anxiety-inducing problems getting to the ground on match day. Waddell had, of course, travelled to Italy to watch Torino playing – both in an away match at Roma and in a vital home win over Internazionale of Milan. The foreign journeys between January's draw and the March first leg were not only about studying the opposition tactics and personnel. Securing such near-perfect locations and facilities was yet another indication of the meticulous preparation the Rangers supremo invested in European matches.

Waddell had other aces up his sleeve and using his inside knowledge of the press-pack, went out of his way to play down the fears of a recurrence of the controversy which had dogged previous Britain v Italy clashes while actually doing all he could to put some pressure on the Torino players and the Swiss referee, Kamber.

On the eve of the game the Ibrox boss declared, 'Everyone knows about the Latin temperament but I don't expect any trouble in this game. Torino are too intent with getting on with the job,' and, he continued along this same tightrope between compliment and gauntlet-laying with, 'Unlike most Italian teams they don't have any prima donnas.' [12]

On the Tuesday evening, the Rangers party enjoyed a useful acclimatisation exercise when they attended the Juventus v Wolves match. This allowed the players to see the stadium they'd be playing in, attune themselves to typical Turin crowd noise and note some characteristics of Italian footballers when faced with British opposition. The Rangers party watched Jim McCalliog, the Scottish internationalist, score for Wolves in a 1-1 draw and Alex MacDonald recalls, 'We watched the Italian fans with their small coffees and that amused us, it wasn't what we were used to back in Scotland. But we also got a bit of the atmosphere that night which was useful.' [13]

Encouragingly for the assembled Rangers team, the sodden Stadio Comunale turf was being steadily cut up by the fast and furious efforts of the players. The chances of the Torino side being able to play a fast-flowing, intricate game within 24 hours were looking bleak. The work ethic which Jock Wallace swore by, literally at times, had seen his charges through many a turgid game on a quagmire pitch so the questions to be asked were of Torino and their ability to adapt.

Regardless of the conditions, both sides prepared differently for the game. All but one of the home side had the luxury of a weekend off. Star man Claudio Sala played for Italy in their friendly international in Athens on the previous Saturday and although the Azzuri lost 2-1 Sala came through the match injury-free. The *granata's* dangerous outside left, Toschi had fully recovered from a back injury. Torino were at full strength and looking to reach a European semi-final for only the second time in their history. [14]

Waddell celebrated his 51st birthday the day before the game with a small champagne reception. The real sense of occasion though, was supplied by the impassioned speech the Rangers boss had made to his players earlier that day. Peter McCloy recalls, 'Waddell spoke to us in the hotel before the game and said that this team were joint-top of the Italian league and teams in the ascendancy like that are dangerous sides to play but he said, if you beat this team you can win the Cup Winners Cup. Get that into your heads!'[15]

The Stadio Comunale was typical of European multi-sports stadiums at that time. [16] If the Rangers players needed further convincing they were on the cusp of European glory, then playing in such a beautiful yet imposing arena would finally hammer the point home. Outside the ground a statue commemorated Italy's two World Cup wins in the thirties and that 1934 tournament was the inspiration behind the design of architect Rafaello Fagnoni's sleekly styled 55,000 capacity super bowl. However, on-field triumphs weren't the only inspiration behind this wonder of pre-stressed concrete construction – it was originally named after the gentleman who opened the stadium, a certain Benito Mussolini! Thankfully, such a grim epithet was not attached for long

to such a beautiful stadium, which is still utilised today as a Juventus training facility while Juve and Torino share the massive Stadio delle Alpi.

Only one cantilevered roof existed on the Comunale and an athletics running track separated the pitch from the first flat parterre concourse of the terracing which sustained three quarters of the ground. [17] But the atmosphere on the night as Torino and Rangers stepped out was nevertheless sensational.

Derek Johnstone had recovered full fitness allowing Rangers to employ the defensive minded 1-4-3-2 formation which most had anticipated. Johnstone played at the heart of defence alongside Colin Jackson. Dave Smith swept up behind as Jardine and Mathieson occupied their usual full-back slots. Across the middle were McLean, MacDonald and Greig with Willie Johnston and Colin Stein, once again, left to do the running up front.

However, that somewhat simple formation was a cause of confusion for some observers. Modern day football fans are used to players wearing squad numbers and the starting eleven can have shirt numbers ranging from 1 to 44 or higher. However, in the early seventies and for a long time after, a number meant a set position and any deviation away from that tradition was deemed suspicious. Thus, the *Glasgow Herald*'s 'Special Correspondent' felt the need to comment on Derek Johnstone playing at centre half, 'despite wearing the number 8 jersey'.[18]

But this traditional midfield shirt number operating in a defensive position highlighted a fairly intrinsic part of Rangers' game plan. Smith, wearing number 6, was the perfect libero, acting as a bolt behind the back four or advancing from behind the defensive curtain to prompt counter-attacks. John Greig, wearing number four, was freed up to play in his left half, midfield role or, more specifically on this occasion, he was let loose on Claudio Sala.[19]

First Leg Torino 1 Rangers 1
8th March 1972
Torino – Castellini, Mozzini, Fossati (Toschi), Zecchin, Cereser, Agroppi, Rampanti (Luppi), Ferrini, Pulici, Sala, Bui. (scorer – Pulici 61)
Rangers – McCloy, Jardine, Mathieson, Greig, Jackson, Smith, McLean, Johnstone, Stein, MacDonald, Johnston. (scorer – Johnston 12)

Greig won the toss and chose to kick-off, then asked Alex MacDonald to knock the ball back to him from the centre-spot, with specific instructions to make the pass a yard or two short. His experiences in Europe with Rangers and in World Cup qualifiers with Scotland had taught John Greig a thing or two about how Italian teams start a game. Sure enough, when Doddie's temptingly truncated pass made its way gently backwards Sala sprinted forward eagerly to gain possession only to

After some rough treatment in Turin, Willie Johnston gets his own back at Ibrox

encounter one of the hardest tackles in European football and a very good reason not to get involved again. Greig looked over to the bench and Waddell could be seen with his head in his hands.[20]

Rangers soon got into a rhythm of possession football which frustrated Torino, who couldn't get their game plan into action. Playing in their all-white European strips with just the circular green, white and red tricolour badge traditionally worn by the Coppa Italia winners, the Turin side became increasingly unrecognisable as the home side. By the twelfth minute the confident start by Rangers was crowned with the opening goal of the night. Willie Mathieson, overlapping down the

First Leg Torino 1 Rangers 1

left wing, beat two Italians and whipped the ball dangerously across the face of the Torino goal. Goalkeeper Castellini got a hand to it but only succeeded in touching the ball into the path of Willie Johnston whose finish was clinical.

The home side tried to respond but Rangers would only allow them to come as far as the 18-yard box and then the defence simply sealed up everything behind it – except Dave Smith. His probing passes out of defence almost never failed to meet the Rangers midfield or the Stein-Johnston double-act up front. Such economy of passing was allowing vital breathing space for the blue rearguard to regroup. Derek Johnstone too was having an immense game for one so young and inexperienced.

In the 24th minute there was a scare for the Scots when a Tommy McLean pass-back was fumbled by McCloy and five minutes from the interval Ferrini went down in the box under the challenge of Derek Johnstone. Referee Kamber waved away the Italian penalty claims and that was that – Rangers went in at half-time with not just a lead but an almost faultless forty five minutes under their belts.

In the second half, however, Torino began to recover from the shock of the determination and class shown by the Scots. The home side mounted ever more threatening attacks and ten minutes after the restart, Peter McCloy failed to hold a Pulici shot but Rangers escaped punishment. The Italians continued to push forward but without success and in 59 minutes outside left Toschi, who was surprisingly left on the bench, replaced left-back Fossati. It took only two minutes for the change to work as Toschi's left foot shot, which McCloy appeared to have covered, was deflected into the net by centre-forward Pulici despite the best efforts of Colin Jackson on the goal-line.

With half an hour remaining it was to be expected that Torino would pile on the pressure especially as they hadn't played for a week while Rangers had been in action on the Saturday. But the best the Italians could manage was a disallowed 'goal' from Pulici and it was they who tired in the face of Rangers' industry and belief. By the end Rangers were playing possession football again, lapping up the jeers and horns from the terraces and almost grabbing another couple of goals through Willie Johnston. It was a superb result, setting the Ibrox men up for the second leg at Ibrox a fortnight later.

An excited Waddell declared Derek Johnstone the new John Charles and Gustavo Giagnoni, the ever gracious Torino coach, gave Rangers two of the biggest compliments the club has ever received. He said the Glasgow men were the fittest team he'd ever seen and that their ultra-defensive approach had been exactly the kind of method employed by Italian teams in European away ties over the years. 'Rangers came here and played the Italian game,' he said.[21]

Barcelona – here we come!

Like their French counterparts previously, the Italian press were less than complimentary but unsurprisingly recognised the Ibrox men's defensive game plan which had been executed almost to perfection. Journalist Bruno Perucca complained about the Scots' rough style of play, claiming that at least one penalty should have been awarded and accused the Swiss referee of leniency. [22]

The players were aware however, of the difficulties still involved in negotiating through to the next round and it's clear that the 'rough' play was not one-sided. Willie Johnston recalls, 'Torino were a good team, no doubt about it. Colin and I played through the middle as usual to try and tie their back four up. The guy I played against was in the tunnel with me at the end of the game. He had kicked me up and down the park as it was but he wasn't happy with that. He was saying to me, Johnston, Johnston, in Glasgow I break your leg. I was just glad big Jock was there alongside me.' [23]

Colin Stein recalled, 'The Italians were more defensively minded and we knew if they got in front then they would just defend. We played well though and it was us who got the first goal. Bud and I did a lot of running about that night as usual and I think we did well to come home with a one each draw.' [24]

Rangers flew home by chartered flight the next morning, arriving in Glasgow at noon, to the news that Celtic too had secured a great result, beating Ujpest Dozsa in Budapest. Yet again the green half of Glasgow wouldn't allow Rangers all the headlines to themselves. Later the same day there was good news for the Ibrox fans when Willie Henderson had amicable talks with Waddell. Interestingly, in a time which had yet to embrace the dubious talents of the football agent, the player's legal representative was a certain Mr Joseph Beltrami – but he was invited to wait outside the manager's office. Henderson agreed to come back to Ibrox on the following Monday to finalise a solution to his previous problems. [25]

The next match on March 11th provided a comfortable 2-0 league win at home to St Johnstone. The goals were scored by Derek Johnstone and Tommy McLean but Waddell was impressed enough by Saints' John Connolly to subsequently make a bid for the left-sided attacker. Rangers' bid of £45,000 was rejected however and the player eventually signed for Everton for £75,000. The increasingly powerful magnet of English football was becoming just too strong.

Sandy Jardine and Colin Stein, as members of a Scottish League side, would travel down to England to play The Football League three days later. With a difficult Scottish Cup quarter-final on the horizon and an equally difficult home match with Torino to follow, this was the last thing Rangers needed. Jardine was captain and Stein scored as the Scots went down 3-2 at Ayresome Park, Middlesborough. While it was undoubtedly an honour for the players, it was probably one they could well have done without in the midst of such a busy schedule. Both men were vital to the Rangers cause and although the inter-league international was a more regular feature of the game in the early seventies, it's still difficult to imagine such key players being released by their clubs in the present day for what was an essentially meaningless fixture.

Indeed Jardine was slow to recover from his efforts on Teesside and this may have been a contributory factor in Rangers' near elimination from the Scottish Cup as the Saturday trip to Fir Park proved as dangerous as had been previously feared. Employing exactly the same defensive personnel and formation as they had in Turin, Rangers found themselves 2-1 down with seven minutes to go in what was a classic cup encounter. Derek Johnstone dropped his defensive duties in a last-ditch effort to save the final vestiges of Rangers' domestic season and Stein equalised to take the tie to a replay. But this was far from the nice, relaxing exercise most teams would prefer in the build-up to a European quarter-final.

Torino, meanwhile, still going strong on the domestic front, beat Fiorentina 2-1 at home the next day while Juventus dropped a point in Naples.

This left Rangers' European opponents three points off the top of Serie A and the fact that they were due to play Juventus the following Sunday had a huge bearing on the debate over subsequent events.

When Torino arrived at Glasgow airport on the Monday creative front-man Claudio Sala and half-back Aldo Agroppi had both been left behind. Furthermore, down in the Midlands, Juventus had arrived for their UEFA cup second leg at Wolverhampton minus the six first team players they'd also left in Turin. Torino coach Giagnoni assured the assembled hacks his side was in Glasgow to win but people began to wonder if the Serie A title-race meant more to the Italian teams than European progress. [26]

The Italians often regard their league title as superior to any European trophy other than the Champions Cup. Furthermore, that famous Italian pragmatism may have decided both Juve and Torino that their 1-1 draws in the home leg of their quarter-finals were not going to be enough to take them through to the semi-finals of Europe or that the effort necessary to achieve the away results in each case would be too damaging to their chances of winning a derby which meant so much more to their *tifosi*.

As life-long Torino fan Mauro Ricci recalls, 'No, Sala wasn't injured. The Torino trainer Giagnoni understood that there was only a small hope, being optimistic, of winning the match in

Glasgow. He preferred to save Sala for the following Sunday's city derby against the 'hunchback zebra' Juventus, accepted as the top match of the season.'[27]

Marco Masoero reaffirmed the parochial nature of Italian football: 'Torino has always been very 'local', deeply rooted in the city's reality, while Juventus has always been a cosmopolitan team. To a typical Torino supporter, defeating Juventus is the most important achievement and in 1971-72 it was the first time, after the Superga disaster of 1949, in which Torino had a concrete opportunity of winning the Italian title – and Juventus was the main challenger!'[28]

But the genial Giagnoni (who would eventually turn up at Rangers' hotel outside Barcelona the day after ultimate victory to congratulate Waddell and drink champagne from the Cup Winners Cup) declared at a pre-match press conference on the Tuesday that his team were, 'Here to work and win. We take our holidays in July.'[29] But the players he was prepared to risk in that effort were not his first-choice line-up.

Arguably the fact that Juventus had been knocked out the UEFA Cup at Molineux on the Tuesday evening was the deciding factor in the selection of the Torino line-up. Perhaps that defeat for Juve told Giagnoni that his team's deadliest rivals were fully focused on the championship race and that he should do likewise. But, whatever the motivation, the fact remains that five of the Torino players who began the first leg in Turin (Mozzini, Zecchin, Sala, Agroppi and Pulici) didn't kick a ball at Ibrox. Luppi played from the start in Scotland after coming on as a 67th minute sub in the Stadio Comunale.

Peter McCloy said, 'We weren't aware of that at the time. We knew they had made some changes but we didn't know if it was forced on them or whatever – we were just totally focused on the game.'[30]

Rangers had travelled down to Largs to prepare for the match after watching a film of the Turin first leg. A potential goalkeeping problem – Peter McCloy was on antibiotics for an infected graze on his thigh – was exacerbated when Bobby Watson fell ill and had to be left at Ibrox. There was a slight worry over Colin Jackson but, in the end, the first choice Rangers team made it onto the pitch for the game which could see the club into the semi-finals of European competition for the fifth time in twelve seasons.

The game itself was, by all accounts, no classic but the occasion, the expectation and hope on the terraces[31] and the finely balanced nature of the tie ensured tension. One goal from Torino and the first-leg advantage Rangers had worked so ferociously to earn, would be wiped out. Instead of being able to go through with a nil-nil, the Ibrox men would then require to score twice against one of the best sides in a league renowned for *catenaccio* defending.

McCloy recalled, 'Waddell said to me

before we went out on to the pitch, Remember if you don't let any goals in we're through. I thought to myself, Thanks very much!'[32]

Second Leg Rangers 1 Torino 0 (Aggregate: Rangers 2 Torino 1)

Second Leg Rangers 1 Torino 0
(Aggregate: Rangers 2 Torino 1)
22nd March 1972
Rangers – McCloy, Jardine, Mathieson, Greig, Jackson, Smith, McLean, Johnstone, Stein, MacDonald, Johnston. (scorer – MacDonald 46)
Torino – Castellini, Lombardo, Fossati (Rossi), Puia, Cereser, Ferrini, Luppi, Crivelli, Bui (Barberes), Rampanti, Toschi.

Rangers took the game to the Italians straight from the kick-off, so much so that *Glasgow Herald* journalist William Hunter described, the next day, how, 'From the start they (Rangers) were looking for goals as if the world was going to end at half-time.'[33]

The home side, despite attacking with vigour and purpose, just couldn't find the guile to penetrate the Torino rearguard and by the end of the first half Rangers looked as though they were beginning to run out of attacking ideas. A John Greig shot which keeper Castellini had to react quickly to save was their only real effort of the half.

For their part, Torino looked sharp and fit but without any real apparent appetite for the task of breaking down a Rangers team so obviously determined. The Italians attacked swiftly when they had possession but, again, Dave Smith was outstanding, breaking-up all incoming attacks before they amounted to anything too serious. There was a scare for Rangers when Bui slipped a pass to Toschi who unleashed a shot past McCloy. Fortunately for the Ibrox men the ball came off the post and the goal remained intact.

However, a minute after the re-start worries were eased a little when Tommy McLean combined with Alex MacDonald for the opener. It was a scrappy goal but it was met with deafening exultation from a packed Ibrox crowd who knew they were another step closer.

McLean remembers the tactical importance of the goal: 'It was nil-nil and a very dour game. The Italians at that time were noted for their counter-attacking system, using the sweeper and catching you on the break so we were always wary. Then we had a flurry right at the start of the second half and I had quite a run – half the length of the park – on the right hand side and I played it across and Alex bundled it over. It was a good start to the second half and it forced them to alter their thinking. The goal gave us a wee bit more leeway and when they came forward we could actually play the game we were quite good at away from home – counter-attacking them.'[34]

As the second half continued Rangers just couldn't get the second goal that would have eased some of the tension and there remained the threat of the conceded goal which would

Barcelona – here we come!

signal the dreaded extra-time and – perhaps even worse – another penalty shoot-out. The Italians had a late flurry of activity but it was all too little too late. Dave Smith, in his assured way, marshalled the defence brilliantly to ensure Rangers went through to their third European Cup Winners Cup semi-final.

The Torino goal under siege in the second leg at Ibrox

Johnston gets a header in despite some close attention from his marker

The Italian press had predicted such an outcome and showed little surprise. They had claimed that Torino had arrived in Glasgow convinced that they were going to be beaten although Rangers were not necessarily superior. Afterwards, *La Stampa* explained that the two Turin sides had both shared a common fate, defeated by British teams partly because they decided not to utilise their best players. [35]

Alex MacDonald scores v Torino at Ibrox to put Rangers into the semi-final

Colin Stein remembers the Italians well. He claims, 'They weren't as flamboyant or had as much flair as the Portuguese in the previous round but they were harder to beat. I remember in the second leg they had a guy with grey hair who was marking me. Every time I ran for a corner, he checked me or stood in front of me. He had all the experience under the sun. It was a clever way to stop me but the boy could play as well. It was a hard game at Ibrox. We had a lot of pressure but they defended well and they were always in the game.'[36]

Willie Johnston recalled, 'The Italians were traditionally well disciplined, you always thought they would just do enough to get by. And Torino were typical, they were a hard side to break down. We were trying to keep the game tight at 1-0 but the fans were pushing us forward. That was always a problem in those days.'[37]

If Torino had kept themselves for the game against Juventus the following Sunday then it succeeded because they beat their great rivals 2-1. However, they failed to win the Championship that season, Juventus ultimately proving too strong. Twice more in the 1970s the Turin giants battled until the last game for the title, Torino eventually winning in 1975/76 but Juventus capturing it back the following season.

Rangers would also go on to win championships in the '70s but their defeat of the Turin side left them with more immediate prospects of success.

Barcelona – here we come!

c h a p t e r

6
BAYERN MUNICH

*The moment young Derek Parlane
made his mark with the Rangers fans*

For once Schwarzenbeck gets the better of Stein

Barcelona – here we come!

'Their heads went down after Derek scored . . . we couldn't believe it.' Alex MacDonald

The defeat of Rennes was quietly efficient, the Sporting Lisbon conquest dramatically entertaining and the Torino victory was tellingly significant. However, the semi-final would demand the truly historic from Rangers as the Ibrox club were paired with the one team they would much rather have left until the final – Bayern Munich. [1] The Germans hadn't yet moved into the new Olympic stadium erected in their home city but the Bavarian Bundesliga specialists were about to enter a new stratosphere in terms of footballing success. [2]

Their key players almost need no introduction. Captain Franz Beckenbauer had not only played in the 1966 and 1970 World Cup finals for West Germany, gaining a runners-up and a third place medal, he'd single-handedly invented the role of the 'libero', the attack-prompting sweeper. Striker Gerd Muller (*der Bomber*) was the top scorer at the 1970 Mexico World Cup, the year he also won the Golden Boot award for top league scorer in Europe and the accolade of the European Footballer of the Year. In 1972, as the two teams prepared to meet, Muller was on his way to winning the Golden Boot for a second time and Beckenbauer, whose reputation continued to grow, would be crowned that season's European Footballer of the Year.

Along with goalkeeper Sepp Maier, defender Georg Schwarzenbeck, midfielder Uli Hoeness and full-back Paul Breitner, Muller and Beckenbauer would go on to form the core of the West Germany team which would win the European Championships so convincingly in June 1972, the World Cup in 1974 and three successive European Cups with Bayern from 1974 to 1976. Rangers were about to play one of the most powerful sides in the annals of the modern game and history was not on their side.

Bayern had thwarted the Ibrox men in the 1967 Cup Winners Cup final in Nuremberg. Infamously playing defender Roger Hynd at centre-forward, Rangers lost by an injury-time goal scored by a certain Franz Roth, a man who would later score the opening goal of a European Cup final in Paris and the only goal of a European Cup final at Hampden.

The defeat at Nuremberg gave this tie a particular resonance for both the Rangers support and a good number of the players. John Greig, Willie Johnston, Dave Smith, Sandy Jardine, Willie Henderson and Ronnie McKinnon played in the game which had become almost as much of a watershed for the club as the infamous 1967 Scottish Cup defeat at Berwick which preceded it by a few months.

In what was effectively a home game for Bayern, the Ibrox players had lost their chance to emulate Celtic's European triumph. Rangers' greatest rivals had won the Champions Cup – at the first attempt – one week before the Nuremberg final. For many Rangers fans, the Cup Winners Cup failure at the hands of Bayern was not only a missed opportunity in terms of furnishing the Ibrox trophy room with a bit of history, but it had allowed Celtic's Lisbon triumph centre stage. However petty it may seem to the outsider it's a feature of close footballing rivalries that success is often measured by what your neighbour achieves. When Celtic pulled off the greatest club triumph any side can achieve the most Rangers could have done was to steal a little of their limelight and perhaps change the perception of that time.

The national and international press may then have meshed together two European trophy wins in the same season – the same week – and Lisbon '67 would forever be associated with Nuremberg '67 in the collective Caledonian football psyche. It would have become known as the week Scottish football had conquered Europe, an increasingly powerful footballing legacy given the famous Scotland victory over the World Champions at Wembley that same season. But it was not to be and the Rangers team who made it through to that 1967 final were soon forgotten.[3]

In addition to the trauma inflicted on the blue half of Glasgow in 1967,

Bayern had only the previous season eliminated their Glaswegian rivals from the Fairs Cup. After going down by a single Beckenbauer goal in Munich, Rangers had subjected Bayern to a barrage in front of more than 80,000 at Ibrox in the second leg. With ten minutes of the tie remaining Bayern managed one of their infrequent attacks and were awarded what the Swiss referee appeared to indicate was an indirect free-kick at the edge of their opponents' box. Gerd Muller stepped up to take the kick and rifled the ball straight into the net, without it touching any player on its way past an unphased Peter McCloy. When the goal was given, however, all hell broke loose, but the referee, Kamber from Switzerland, was adamant and the goal stood. Rangers went straight up the pitch and equalised on the night through Colin Stein but still required another two goals in the space of eight minutes if they wanted to qualify. There was little hope of that and the Ibrox men's European involvement was over for another season.[4]

So there were issues between the two teams. However, the prospect of another titanic battle was put on hold as the league campaign had still to be attended to, although it was becoming abundantly clear that Rangers were merely playing out the season. The Saturday after eliminating Torino, the Ibrox men, albeit weakened, somehow managed to lose 2-1 at home to Morton. The fans also seemed to accept

Barcelona – here we come!

that the domestic season was over, as only 20,00 turned up to see the match.[5]

The Scottish Cup quarter-final replay against Motherwell came only two days later and the line-up which put Torino out of the Cup Winners Cup quarter-final, put the Lanarkshire men out of the Scottish Cup quarter-final, 4-2, ensuring that April would be the month of the semi-finals.

Waddell and Wallace's team selections seemed to indicate Rangers were experimenting tactically and resting key players during league matches before bringing them back for the Cup competitions. Again, the management team's tacit acceptance of the league championship failure that season can be counterbalanced with their determination to ensure the club won in Europe and thus throws up a strange scenario. How many Scottish clubs in the present day would 'decide' to win a European trophy to appease themselves and their fans until they were ready to challenge for the SPL title? Of course, it would have been interesting to observe the fall-out if the Ibrox 'plan' had come unstuck.

After the four month wait between the Sporting and Torino ties, Rangers had a mere fortnight between the quarters and semi-finals. Having played Torino, Morton and Motherwell, all at Ibrox, in the space of five days, they were due yet another home encounter on Saturday April 1st, against Ayr United, before flying out to Munich for the first leg.

With the Fairs Cup match having taken place only eighteen months earlier, Bayern were bound to feel they had the upper-hand psychologically. They'd never lost to Rangers over ninety minutes in matches home, away or in a 'neutral' stadium. However, Sandy Jardine was not fearful. He said, 'We respected them but we weren't scared of them. Although we hadn't beaten them we had always put up a good show and the games were always close. They had never given us a going over.'[6]

On the day of the Ayr United match, Jock Wallace travelled to watch Bayern defeat Cologne 3-0 in a German Cup quarter-final while Waddell was left to hope all his players would get through the match against the Somerset Park men. John Greig and Tommy McLean were already out due to injuries sustained in the Motherwell replay and remained slightly doubtful for the first leg against Bayern. While the outside right had a niggling rib injury, the club captain's leg was in a slightly more worrying condition.

Waddell needed a break on the injury front and his prayers were partly answered when an old-fashioned Scottish downpour caused the postponement of the Ayr match. Instead of competitive action the players were put through a full training routine at the Albion training ground to keep them ticking over. By the Monday neither Greig nor McLean, who had both received further treatment on their injuries, were totally out of the woods but Waddell included both in his squad of nineteen for Germany:

McCloy, Jardine, Mathieson, Greig, Jackson, Smith, McLean, Conn, D Johnstone, Stein, A MacDonald, W Johnston, Neef, Denny, Miller, Parlane, Penman, Fyfe, I MacDonald.

The Rangers players trained on the Monday but the Bayern players had the day off due to the fact that, whereas Rangers played no football that week-end, the Bundesliga side had engaged in not one but two matches. Their 3-0 German Cup victory over Cologne on the Saturday was followed up by a long-held commitment to travel to Paris and play an exhibition match against Benfica of Portugal. There's little doubt this match had been treated as nothing other than a friendly and played at a pace to suit but it smacked of complacency and over confidence.

In addition, the aforementioned core six of Maier, Breitner, Beckenbauer, Schwarzenbeck, Hoeness and Muller had all played in West Germany's 2-0 friendly win over Hungary in Budapest the previous Wednesday. Hoeness and Breitner scored the goals that night. This West German national team were in the quarter-finals of the European Championship tournament and looking unstoppable. Bayern had just eased into the semi-finals of their national cup competition and the previous Saturday's victory in Stuttgart put them

top of the Bundesliga for only the second time that season.[7] And Rangers stood in their way of another Cup Winners Cup final appearance. The gang of six, the bedrock of the Bayern and West German team were brimming with confidence but had played three matches in three different countries during a week in which Rangers had rested.

Based ten miles from Munich, in a Bavarian woodland hotel, Rangers were allowed to use Bayern's marvellously modern training facilities. It was there on the Tuesday, that the psychological brinkmanship began in earnest. John Greig recalls Waddell bursting into the treatment room followed by a pack of the German press and pointing to his captain's exposed cuts and bruises and declaring, 'This is Greig, the captain of Rangers, and he'll be playing tomorrow night despite those injuries.'[8] While Greig remained unsure as to what exactly was going on, it seemed Waddell was using his personal experience of the press to exploit a photo and headline opportunity which would let the Bayern players know just exactly how committed their opponents were feeling. Greig himself suddenly realised he would now have little choice but to get himself fit for the following evening!

The Rangers manager's opposite number, Udo Lattek, was some fourteen years younger but had been manager only three months less than Waddell.[9] Where Waddell sought to

Barcelona – here we come!

intimidate, Lattek used modesty and self-deprecation in an effort to lull Rangers into a false sense of superiority. The German said, 'I think we will win by one goal. I just hope it is enough to take to Glasgow. Rangers were most unlucky to lose to us last year.' [10]

His two most influential players were even more condescending. Beckenbauer feigned bleak pessimism with, 'We will need at least a three-goal lead to take to Ibrox. . . I just do not see it happening for Rangers are a very good side.' [11] And Muller went completely over the top, saying, 'I think we can win by one goal in Munich but I honestly feel Rangers will get to the final and go on to win the cup in Barcelona.' [12] However, the light-hearted nature of the German's training session which preceded the press conference pointed to a confident Munich camp.

Looking back from the present day, where tactics are of crucial importance in the game, the attitude of Waddell, who, remember, was something of tactical pioneer at that time, is remark-able. His only comment as to how Rangers would tackle one of the most brilliant teams in World football was stunningly simple, almost dismissive, 'We will have to adapt ourselves against Bayern. . . they have to take the initiat-ive and while the basic tactics will be laid down shortly before kick-off, it may very well rest with the players themselves on how to handle the Germans.' [13]

His summation of Bayern's tactics were similarly basic, 'They may decide that Beckenbauer should come forward. . . or they may play him as a straight-forward sweeper. That's where the adapting comes in on the part of the players.' [14]

First Leg
Bayern Munich 1 Rangers 1
5th April 1972

Lattek would field the same team that defeated Cologne in the German Cup. Maier, Hansen, Breitner, Schwarzenbeck, Beckenbauer, Roth (Schneider), Krauthausen, Zobel, Muller, Hoeness, Suchnholz. (scorer – Breitner 23)

Waddell announced his starting eleven – it would be the same as that which defeated Torino at Ibrox: McCloy, Jardine, Mathieson, Greig, Jackson, Smith, McLean, Johnstone, Stein, MacDonald, Johnston. (scorer – Zobel o.g. 49)

The Rangers players who appeared that night are unified in the assertion that they were given the biggest maul-ing of their lives in the opening half hour of a game which, incredibly, they eventually drew. Within eight minutes Gerd Muller had headed against Peter McCloy's upright and wave after wave of Bayern attacks over the next quarter of an hour eventually saw the home side take an inevitable lead.

Tommy McLean remembers it well, 'I was back defending with the rest of the team. I challenged Breitner away down in his left-back corner and he played a wee one-two past me and he ran the length of the park, played it across to the right wing. It came back into the middle and he side-footed it in from about six yards.' [15]

The poor start didn't augur well for the Scots but the never-say-die attitude of the Rangers team and a healthy chunk of good fortune, helped them weather the rest of the first half storm. Disciplined play with Colin Jackson's tight marking of the lethal Gerd Muller and Derek Johnstone's refusal to let playmaker Uli Hoeness out of his sight, meant that by half time the visitors had a more solid foothold in the game.

Jackson recalls the difficult task he had with Muller. He said, 'You had to be on your toes all the time. He was a better version of Joe Harper, a low centre of gravity and as strong as an ox. And he stuck his backside out like Dalglish and could turn you left or right, so you couldn't get too close to him. He would drift out of the game to give the impression he was disinterested and also drift into positions where he could get back into the focus of the attack straight away. In Scotland the strikers would come straight at you and want to be involved in the game all the time. 90% of the time the ball wouldn't go near Muller but the final touch was always his.' [16]

Three minutes into the second half Rangers made the breakthrough which inspired one of the most significant results in the club's history. Ibrox fans may better remember the second leg victory over Bayern at Ibrox but when Stein and Johnston broke from the centre circle towards the Bayern goal in 49 minutes of the first leg, the truly crucial goal of the tie was imminent.

Stein recalls, 'I got into their box, went round Maier and whacked it across and Zobel put it right into the corner of the net.' [17] Yet again Rangers had scored in the away leg. After the trauma of Lisbon, the Ibrox players were not likely to forget the significance of an away goal and it wasn't lost on Bayern either. They were shattered. As breathtakingly as they had begun the match, the German threat gradually died.

The defensive pressures eased to the extent that Willie Mathieson could advance from his full-back berth and indulge himself with a couple of dangerous shots on the Bayern goal. The tables had turned and by the end of the match Rangers were unlucky not to have actually snatched victory.

Tommy McLean laughs as he remembers, 'In the last minute we could actually have won the game because one of Peter's long kick-outs, similar to the one in the Moscow Dynamo game, gave us a chance. Their centre-half misheaded it and wee Willie Johnston went through with only the goalie to beat – and the referee blew for time up! It was ridiculous but to be fair it would have been more outrageous if we had won the game after that first-half mauling.' [18]

Barcelona – here we come!

Why the sudden turnaround after the break? Sandy Jardine is in no doubt: 'Our fitness began to tell and they wilted. The first half was the biggest doing I'd ever been involved in but we'd only lost the one goal. They came at us again in the second half for fifteen minutes but we weathered that storm and by the end of the game we could have won it. Our fitness told and we over-ran them at the end'. [19]

Stein concurs, 'They murdered us in the first half. They hemmed us in and we couldn't get out of our own half. In saying that we defended resolutely because we could easily have folded under the pressure. We came back into the game later and finished really strong. We were a fit team then and that's what got us through those games.' [20]

Willie Johnston has other memories of that night. He laughed, 'That was the night when young Jim Denny got the nickname Pele. After the game Colin and me were knackered and we were sitting, not standing, in the showers. Jim came in to hurry us up but we were too tired to move. I said to him, What about that Beckenbauer, he's some player isn't he? And Jim said, Aye, but he can only kick with one foot. And he was serious! We were laughing and started calling him Pele after that.' [21]

Rangers became only the fifth away side to escape Bayern's Grünwalder Strasse ground undefeated in a European tie and the Scottish press were kind to the Ibrox team. The

Glasgow Herald's 'Special Correspondent' claimed 'another victory for Rangers' tactics. From the start they were more aggressive than in the last round against Torino and never allowed this German side to settle into their normal fluid rhythm.' [22]

But Bayern could still afford to feel confident. In the previous three rounds they'd accounted for Skoda Plzen of Czechoslovakia, Bill Shankly's emerging Liverpool and Steau of Bucharest by performing well away from home. They'd actually won both ties against the Czechs, gained a goal-less draw at Anfield and finished one goal apiece in Bucharest. Although the Rangers tie was the first of the tournament in which they played the away leg second, Bayern knew they were more than capable of getting the minimum one goal they needed to stay in the competition.

Also, the visit to Scotland was not a jaunt into the unknown. The game at Ibrox the previous season had been watched by 80,000 and Maier, Beckenbauer and Muller had all played for the West German national side which drew 1-1 with Scotland at Hampden in April 1969 in front of 110,000. Therefore the Germans knew what to expect.

If further evidence was required to prove that Rangers were far from assured a place in their third European final, it was provided just three days later when both sides returned to their respective domestic duties. A Rangers team showing only two changes from the Munich line up (Derek Parlane and Graham Fyfe coming in for Colin Stein and Alex MacDonald) could only muster a 1-1 draw at relegation-bound Clyde. On the Monday, a 2-0 defeat at Dundee was further evidence of the late season league slump. Bayern, on the other hand, scored four goals in the first half hour of their match against mid-table Werder Bremen and eventually won 6-2 with Muller getting a hat-trick. [23] It seemed the Germans' game plan had kicked in three days too late!

The following weekend saw Rangers prepare to grab their last chance for domestic success in the Scottish Cup semi-final against Hibs. However, before the game a virus swept through the Rangers camp and with half the team prescribed antibiotics, it was hardly ideal preparation and it got worse. Only two hours before kick-off Sandy Jardine had complained of feeling unwell and Waddell literally stopped the bus which was taking the reserve team to East End Park, Dunfermline in order to plunder a few back-ups for his ailing first-team squad. Then during the match itself, further disaster occurred when John Greig sustained an ankle injury and after half an hour in which he tried to play through an agonising pain barrier, despite the pleadings from the bench, he eventually relented and was replaced by Jim Denny. It's indicative of Greig's standing that he himself decided when he was coming off.

In what was never the greatest of games, Alex MacDonald put Rangers ahead three minutes before half-time only to see Jim O'Rourke equalise three minutes after the break. Considering the illness and injury problems, Waddell was pleased enough to earn a replay but any sense of accomplishment was undermined by other events. While Rangers were being held at Hampden, Celtic were tying up a record-breaking seventh successive league title in Methil against East Fife. The pressure on Rangers to make something of their season was greater than ever.

The Scottish Cup replay was put on hold as Rangers retreated to their Largs base to prepare for their European semi-final second leg against Bayern and, just a few miles down the Ayrshire coast, Celtic resided at Seamill before the home leg of their Champions Cup semi-final against their old foes Internazionale of Milan. Having drawn 0-0 in the San Siro, Celtic, like Rangers, were favourites to go on to their third European final. It was 1967 all over again.

There was a high-level of anticipation in Glasgow. With an 80,000 all-ticket sell-out at Ibrox and a 75,000 all-ticket sell-out at Parkhead, plus the millions watching on TV, it was going to be quite a night. The staggered kick-off times of the two matches ensured STV could show the whole ninety minutes of Rangers v Bayern Munich and, providing the Ibrox match didn't go to extra time, then show the last half hour of the Celtic v Inter game. The BBC intended, somewhat strangely, to screen only the last half hour of the Parkhead game. [24]

Retrospectively, the pre-match comments of both the press and the Rangers manager, given the magnitude of the game, seem amazingly low-key. There is no hint of the historic nature of the occasion, only journalist Jim Parkinson's notion that, 'Rangers, paradoxically, have increased certain tactical pressures on themselves for this return match.' He asked of the Ibrox team, 'Do they base their plans on a no-scoring draw, thus winning on a technicality, or do they go all-out for clean cut victory and leave themselves exposed against such world class players?' [25] It seems incredible, looking back, that in the early seventies a win on away goals rule was regarded, by Parkinson anyway, as winning 'on a technicality' almost as though it was ignoble when compared to the 'clean-cut' victory. [26]

As the toss-of-a-coin method of deciding tied European matches was still very prevalent in the psyche of football people in 1972, the away-goals rule, being its replacement, would be regarded with some of the same scepticism. How times have changed. If a Scottish team were to progress into a European final nowadays there would be no-one in any way troubled as to how they got there. It's almost quaint now to recall Willie Waddell's insistence that in maintaining their advantage from the first leg, Rangers shouldn't, 'spoil the spectacle'. [27]

In Largs the outbreak of illness continued and everything possible was done to alleviate it with the club doctor attending to Jardine, Stein, Johnston, MacDonald and McLean. Greig's ankle was giving grave cause for concern but, after arranging for x-rays which showed deep bruising rather than any breaks, Waddell ordered his captain to undergo intensive heat treatment at Ibrox. He-rejoined the squad at Largs and, in what was a traditional method of healing, he was ordered into the Firth of Clyde to give his ankle some salt-water treatment. On the Saturday Greig had no chance of playing – by the Wednesday morning it had improved to an even money chance. The news-papers speculated about who would replace Greig if he didn't make it with the only candidates mentioned being Jim Denny and Alfie Conn.

Waddell didn't discuss the tactics until the players arrived back at Ibrox from Largs just a few hours before kick off. Greig hadn't recovered and to the astonishment of the press and most Rangers fans, the club captain was replaced by neither Denny nor Conn but by 19 year-old Derek Parlane. As with Derek Johnstone in the 1970/71 Old Firm League Cup final, Waddell showed amazing faith in a young unproven player. Parlane was actually a few months older than Johnstone but at barely nineteen this was another gamble. Again, it paid off spectacularly.[28]

Second Leg Rangers 2 Bayern Munich 0 (Aggregate: Rangers 3 Bayern Munich 1)

19th April 1972

Rangers – McCloy, Jardine, Mathieson, Parlane, Jackson, Smith, McLean, Johnstone, Stein, MacDonald, Johnston. (scorers – Jardine 1, Parlane 23) Bayern – Maier, Hansen, Breitner (Rybarczyk), Schwarzenbeck, Beckenbauer, Roth, Schneider, Zobel, Muller, Hoeness, Koppenhofer.

Rangers got off to a great start from which the Germans never recovered. A mere forty five seconds were on the clock when Willie Johnston's cross from the left caused mayhem in the German defence. Beckenbauer couldn't clear his lines properly and Derek Johnstone picked up the ball before feeding Jardine who had positioned himself in the inside right channel. The right back tried his luck with a shot which could best be described as 'sclaffed' but to his and the supporters' amazement, Maier let the ball drift past him and into the corner of the net. The keeper had obviously thought the ball was going wide but his mistake had been costly. He might have heard his teammates' less than complimentary thoughts if 80,000 Rangers fans hadn't exploded with joy. It was the perfect start and the Scots went from strength to strength.

Again Colin Jackson shackled Muller so well that the German was forced to go scavenging back into his own half looking for a kick of the ball. Derek Johnstone, showing maturity beyond his years, once again smothered the creative talents of Uli Hoeness. Young Parlane frustrated the experienced Franz Roth – scorer of the only goal in that 1967 Nuremberg final – and Dave Smith, captain for the night, was nothing short of majestic as he showed Beckenbauer there were other liberos in the world who could do the job with the same calmness and assurance.

Rangers sensed the visitors were there for the taking. Stein was unlucky not to double the Ibrox men's lead when he headed against the post but there was an inevitability about the second goal which came after only 23 minutes – although the scorer was something of a surprise. A Johnston corner from the left was contested by the vulnerable Maier and the challenging Stein. The ball was knocked out to the waiting Parlane, 14 yards out, who slid in to volley the ball in off the crossbar as the Germans stood rooted to the spot, stunned. The youngster had vindicated Waddell's gamble.

At the beginning of the second half, Hoeness escaped the shadow of Johnstone to fire in a shot which McCloy pushed onto the post and with that, the German threat disintegrated, along with their discipline. With West Germany's national team coach, Helmut Schoen, watching from the main stand, Beckenbauer, Maier, Muller, Hoeness *et al* began to bicker between themselves. The team who were about to dominate the European game, with the players who would form the heart of the best international side in the world, were frustrated in the face of Rangers superiority. Waddell's men were truly ready for a European final.

Alex MacDonald remembers, 'The park wasn't too good and Beckenbauer was trying to play the ball with the outside of his foot and it was going out for a shy. So he was getting frustrated. Their heads went down after Derek scored and we couldn't believe it. Their famous names didn't stop me from trying to wind them up or put them off and they didn't like our fitness that night – we were strong and sharp.'[29]

Colin Stein said, 'They were disappointing at Ibrox although Beckenbauer was still obviously a great player and it was difficult to get near him. Mind you, he swore at me, in English, when I kicked him on the ankle. He was so frustrated and I knew then we had them. Schwarzenbeck was their centre half and I gave him a roasting in the last 20 minutes. I enjoyed that.'[30]

Colin Jackson remembers, 'In the second half, down at the Copland Road end, Maier was getting pelters from Beckenbauer just as we were about to take a corner kick. Then Beckenbauer just turned and walked out of the six-yard box and right out of the penalty area altogether, like a big kid in a huff. He didn't want to know! But Beckenbauer was very intimidating even from

*Second Leg
Rangers 2
Bayern Munich 0
(Aggregate:
Rangers 3 Bayern
Munich 1)*

Alex MacDonald, surrounded by Koppenhofer, Breitner and Roth, gets in a shot on the Bayern goal

Beckenbuaer watches in dismay as Parlane (on ground) shoots Rangers into the European Cup Winners Cup final

the other end of the park. He was different class and strutted about the pitch even more than Baxter. He was an excellent player.'[31]

Johnston has his own particular memories of that game: 'Once we scored that early goal I knew there was no way we would get beat. But they kept giving me the ball that night and I ran myself into the ground on the wing, putting the ball past their right back. At the end I launched the ball into the crowd to get a rest. One of the other guys said, What are you doing? I said, I'm knackered – and if you pass that ball to me again it's going in the same place!'[32]

Tommy McLean felt the Germans' performance to be anti-climatic: 'Well, we got the two goal lead and then it was the case that the German mentality disappointed us because, really, they're the ones who were always portrayed as ruthlessly efficient. There was a lot of petulance in their team – players falling

out with each other – they lacked a bit of fight. We expected a wee bit more from them.'[33]

Not that the Ibrox hordes were too concerned about the Germans' deficiencies. As they sensed another final appearance, the new terrace anthem *Barcelona, here we come!* grew from a whisper to a roar. The fans cheered the team through to the final whistle with a confidence not normal in European semi finals.

Across the city, Celtic were having a very different sort of night. The Rangers players watched on a TV in the carnival atmosphere of the home dressing room as the Parkhead men lost on penalties to Inter. The Italians had avenged their 1967 defeat by Celtic as Rangers had avenged their '67 defeat by Bayern.

Of course Celtic's defeat was an added bonus for the Ibrox fans. Billy McMahon recalls, 'After the Rangers game finished we were back in the Halfway Bowling Green in time to see the last five minutes of extra-time at Parkhead. When Dixie Deans put his penalty kick over the bar, the roof nearly came off. What a night that was. I got home the next morning, I think.'[34]

Garry Lynch said, 'I was in a car dropping off a friend in Carmyle when we heard on the radio that Dixie Deans had missed his penalty and Celtic were out. I thought that was quite ironic given that Dixie came from Carmyle. In truth, it would have been better for Scottish football if both teams had reached the final, but sod that!'[35]

Barcelona – here we come!

c h a p t e r

7

THE FINAL

RANGERS
V
MOSCOW
DYNAMO

Nou Camp, Barcelona - the venue for the 1972 final

Barcelona – here we come!

'I turned away to celebrate and there was nothing but Rangers fans on the park.' Colin Stein

Rangers players, officials and fans awoke after the Bayern victory to discover their opponents in their third European final would be yet another old foe, Moscow Dynamo. The Russians had overcome Dynamo Berlin in the other semi-final tie.

The final on May 24th was still some weeks away and the Ibrox men had a fast declining league campaign to complete with a domestic lifeline in the shape of the Scottish Cup semi-final replay. As preparation for their biggest game in five seasons, it was an unmitigated disaster.

After beating the mighty Germans on the Wednesday, the Ibrox men's confidence was high enough to follow it up with a comfortable 3-0 away win at Airdrie. But the domestic disarray soon returned. The Scottish Cup replay against Hibs at Hampden two days later gave Rangers their last chance of domestic success. However, a lifeless Rangers went down 2-0 to a team who would then go on to get annihilated 6-1 by Celtic in the final.

The Ibrox players and fans had, subconsciously at least, turned their attentions away from the League campaign, looking ahead to Barcelona. Peter McCloy recalls, 'Everyone was totally focused on the final, so I wouldn't say the players were exactly throwing themselves into tackles. That obviously showed in the league results and I think it was only tolerated by the fans because the final was coming up.'[1]

Three home games finished off the league campaign. The following Saturday at Ibrox Dunfermline beat the home side by 4 goals to 3 watched by a crowd of only 5000 – the home supporters were clearly saving their money for Spain. Then Rangers capitulated 2-1 to Hibs before a May Day 4-2 victory over Ayr United, their league send-off witnessed by a paltry crowd of 4000. Many inside Ibrox that day may have commented on the news that Willie Henderson, after a season of indecision and turmoil, had been freed. Rangers kept themselves ticking over with a testimonial match in Inverness and a Charity game against St Mirren at Love Street. The matches also allowed John Greig to make a couple of appearances in his bid to prove his fitness.

But these games, important as they were to the players, merely prolonged the agony for the Rangers fans who had had Barcelona on their minds since the night of the Bayern victory.

The cosmopolitan Catalonian capital, in its present condition, is arguably the most perfect setting for a European final and undoubtedly added to the drama and sense of occasion of Manchester United's famous victory

A Moscow Dynamo supporter explains his side's route to the final

We Dynamo supporters of the late '60s and early '70s were sure that our team could win any match, cup or tournament. Dynamo history – great Dynamo history – taught us that. We were the first champions of the country, the first team to do the double and our team opened the European horizons for Soviet football with great tours in the UK in 1945 and Sweden in 1948.

Our last title had been won in 1963 although we won the Cup twice in 1967 and in 1970. The last victory gave us, at last ,the chance to play in Europe. But we should have started earlier, in 1968. The first Soviet team who played in European tournaments was Dynamo Kiev, who made the quarter-finals of the Cup Winners Cup in 1965.

Then Moscow Torpedo played against the defending European Cup holders Inter Milan in 1966, and Dynamo Kiev beat the defending champions Celtic in 1967. But none of the Soviet teams could win in early Spring and pass the quarter-finals barrier.

We were sure that Moscow Dynamo as regular Soviet football trailblazers would do it. And waited for the start of European football in 1968, when we had to play in the Cup Winners Cup in Malta. We had a really brilliant team at that time, but the Soviet Army and other Warsaw Treaty Armies entered Czechoslovakia, and the draw was reorganised in such a way that socialist teams had to play among themselves in the first round. But for political reasons practically all East-European teams withdrew from the Cups. So we had to wait for our start for three more years.

But time did not spare our brilliant team. Yashin, Chislenko and some other great players had quit, new players came and some of them were also great – like Kozlov or Gershkovich, but. . . they lacked the guts and the character of real winners.

We were lucky in the draw. Our opponents were by no means the elite teams of Europe (with one exception – Red Star from Yugoslavia) and we played all first legs away. Our first tie was against Olympiakos from Greece. Two goals from Kozlov in the away match left no doubts who the winner would be. At home the Greeks scored early, we equalised and then the Greeks scored again. The last minutes of the game were very unnerving. After that night Dynamo fans used to shout O-LYM-PIA-KOS when they were not satisfied with the team.

Then was Eskishehirspor from Turkey and two 1-0 victories saw us through to the Spring of 1972.

We had our doubts about our future in the Cup before the first game against the Yugoslavs. It was not televised so we followed it on the radio and we won 2-1. At that time they did not play football in Moscow in March and April as it was too cold and the pitches were unplayable. So our home games were played in southern cities of the country and we watched them only on television. A 1-1 draw in Tashkent was enough for us to be the first Soviet team in a European semi-final.

We were lucky again and drew Dynamo Berlin. We played much better in the first game in Berlin, were ahead 1-0, but our new star Kozhemyakin caught the ball in his hands in the penalty box after he thought he had heard the referee's whistle! They scored but a 1-1 draw in the away match was not bad. Our home game was played in Lvov and again I watched on TV. The game was very tough and hard, a real struggle and we drew 1-1 again. Everything was to be decided in a penalty shoot-out. We Dynamo supporters were calm. We could not miss our chance to be the first. And we didn't. [2]

over Bayern Munich in 1999. However, in 1972, the Nou Camp was just a name and meant little to the ordinary Ibrox die-hards, most of whom had yet to sample the delights of foreign travel.

Jordi Robisoro, a resident of Barcelona said, 'Culturally, this is now an incredible city but it has changed tremendously in the last thirty years. In 1972 there were few tourists here. When Franco died a few years later it was an opening for many people in Barcelona and since the Olympics in 1992 there has been an explosion in tourism.'[3]

The Rangers supporters, flushed with the excitement of a European final, treated the trip as the ultimate summer holiday. Jack Bain recalls, 'I was the convenor of a supporters' club in Burnbank and the Saturday after the Bayern semi-final, we were all down the pub and someone came in saying he had just booked up for three days in Barcelona for, I think £42. So we all rushed up to book our trip. Later on, somebody else came in saying they had got five days for a few quid more. So we all hurried back to change our bookings.'[4]

John Miller remembers, 'My wife had a knitting machine and you would have thought our group were dressed for the Olympics. We had the blue blazers, grey flannels, white jumpers with the red and blue at the neck. The Provident man came to the door and he was a Rangers fan and he was going, so I knew I was going to be okay for a loan.

I worked in Langside bus garage and seven of us were going, which caused a problem in itself, and we all got Provvy cheques. It was £5 cheques and I remember the Provvy man in my kitchen counting out eleven of them for the cost of my trip. He was laughing of course because he was on commission.'[5]

Billy McMahon, another veteran of Barcelona said, 'There was about a dozen of us from our club in Cambuslang who went and it was to be my first time outside Britain. The only people who had been abroad at that time were soldiers and sailors! I worked in the local power station alongside a lot of guys that had been in the Navy and I had listened to them for years talking about being abroad. So yes, I was excited.'[6]

The Scottish press, understandably more blasé about foreign travel, focused on the potential for trouble. It was almost expected. Alex Cameron in the *Daily Record* said the Spanish police, 'cannot believe that Scottish supporters are as bad as has been reported to them' and went on to say, 'Every Scot must hope that Rangers win their battle. And that the fans don't try to start one of their own!'[7]

The hey-day of football hooliganism had not yet begun but the Ibrox fans had a less than spotless reputation, especially on their travels. There had been trouble in Wolverhampton in an earlier European campaign and the riot at St James's Park in 1969, when Rangers were beaten by Newcastle

United, were still fresh in everyone's minds. Therefore, Cameron had every right to flag up his concerns and there were others who were equally apprehensive.

The British consul in Barcelona, Ron Juchan, was less than enthusiastic about the imminent Scottish invasion and talked about the, 'fiasco of Lisbon in 1967 – we still recall the shambles'. Seven hundred Celtic fans had to be repatriated and Juchan complained that five years later, 'some had still to pay their money back'.[8]

Dr Grace Thornton, British Consul in Lisbon in 1967 was as disenchanted by her experience as her colleague. 'Celtic fans? Don't mention them to me. I don't want to see a single one for the rest of my life.'[9]

Juchan went on to say ominously, 'What people coming here must remember is that Spanish police are very tough policemen indeed. They stand no nonsense, not from their own folk or from anyone else. Drunks are rarely seen here and are treated with great contempt.'[10]

The Chief of Police in Barcelona, Sergio Gomez Alba revealed a darker attitude saying, 'I am worried about my own people. There are some who might use the match to make political demonstration.' He talked almost excitedly of sending in his troops to clear out the undesirables in the city centre area of Barrio Chino adding, 'the feeling is the locals will tend to support the Russians. They came here a year ago to play a friendly and the people took them to their hearts. In this part of Spain there are people who are left wing like the Russians.'

But whatever political bond existed was hardly reciprocated from the Soviets. A puzzled Alba said, 'We have not heard one word from them. We don't know what their plans are, when they are coming, how many fans will be here, nothing.'[11]

The Spanish press played it low key, not giving it the comprehensive hype we would nowadays expect from a country hosting a major European final. But if nothing else, as in the case of the French and German press previously, there was some curious national stereotyping going on.

Josef Playa in the *El Correo* commented on Rangers manager Willie Waddell abruptly leaving a press conference, 'The British can do without most things but certainly not their food and 5 o'clock tea.'[12] Playa also noted that Rangers players at training were, 'white and freckled. . . with very red faces, especially after exercise and abundant curly red hair.'[13]

Due to the Cold War politics of the time, like most westerners, the Ibrox fans knew little about the Soviet Union or its football. They knew that Rangers had faced the Russians in 1945 after the war in the famous 2-2 friendly at Ibrox and that, coincidentally, the two teams had met in another friendly the season before when a Derek Johnstone goal had separated the two sides. But, on

Barcelona – here we come!

the other hand, the Russians were better informed about their opponents.

Dynamo fan Ded Borzov recalls, 'We Russians are curious which is why we knew everything about Rangers. We knew that they played twice in Cup Winners Cup finals and once in the European Cup semi-final. We also knew that they, together with Celtic, were the unchallengeable champions of Scotland. We had also heard about the religious aspect of your derbies with Celtic. But all that taken in consideration, we did not consider Glasgow Rangers seriously. . . the general mood was that we were lucky with the quality of our opponents and to take the Cup would be a mere formality.'[14]

Muscovite Sergei Markov also remembers, 'Dynamo fans knew a lot about Scottish football. We remembered the brilliant 3-2 victory over England – the World Champions – in 1967. We also remembered Celtic had been European Cup winners. So Glasgow Rangers, the great rivals of Celtic and one of the two Scotch (*sic*) giants, were a team that should be respected. And respect we had, but no fear. Before the final we all considered our chances as 50/50. One of my pals promised to walk with the Dynamo banner from the Dynamo stadium down to the Red Square if we won – an unthinkable thing in those times.'[15]

So in blissful ignorance of their opponents, the Rangers fans embarked on what was described as 'the biggest airlift Scottish football has ever known'.[16] According to the British Consulate, Rangers had been given 27,000 tickets and 62 chartered flights left Scotland bound for Spain.[17] In addition, numerous supporters buses and private cars made their way over land and sea to Barcelona.

Jack Bain recalls, 'We travelled in the clothes we wore in Scotland – jumpers, cardigans and long trousers. We saw guys boarding the plane at Prestwick

The Rangers dugout in Barcelona - not an ideal place to watch the game

Rangers fans in fine voice before the final in Barcelona

taken their flags down in case they got stolen. It was an amazing atmosphere. I had been to Wembley about five time previous to that and that was the best stadium I had been in until then. But the landscaped entry, the occasion, the weather, we were in awe of it all.'[19]

John Powell recalls an eventful trip, 'I was 17 years old when I travelled to Barcelona with a friend. This was our first trip abroad with Rangers and it was on a privileged ticket from British Rail. We did belong to the Sunnyside Rangers Supporters' Club in Coatbridge but we had decided to do it alone. We were the envy of many of our mates and felt on top of the world when we left on that Sunday evening. The journey was quite eventful – imagine a thirteen-coach train out of Glasgow Central full of Gers fans. We arrived in London the next morning, did a little sightseeing and gave the Londoners a sight to see! Paris was fun, just looking at the sights, drinking in the cafes and generally feeling good. We boarded a night train to Port Bou and changed for Barcelona for the last part of the journey.

'We had a marvellous time on the Tuesday mixing with the local people who received us well and the weather was glorious. Of course the general atmosphere of the city was amazing and the hordes of generally well behaved fans added to this. We made our way to the Nou Camp about 5pm and absorbed the amazing atmosphere with everybody in fine voice. To us this was a dream come true – Rangers in a Euro

with their coats on and collars and ties! When we got there it was so hot we had to go and buy vests and shorts from a local market. But everything was so cheap so it wasn't a big deal. As we approached Barcelona before the game I was struck by the slums on the outskirts of the city, they were like shanty towns.'[18]

Billy McMahon remembers, 'There were pipers there, from up north, Inverness or Elgin, and there were fans with kilts on. When we got to the airport they were handing out blue and white hats and lion rampants, good cloth ones not paper ones. I know the Boys Brigade flag got taken off its pole in Cambuslang and they brought it back after the game. The bowling greens had

Barcelona – here we come!

final in one of the finest cities in the world.'[20]

Jim Shirkie recalls, 'I had only just moved to Thringstone in Leicestershire a year earlier and there were about six of us from the Rangers Supporters' Club who flew out from Heathrow on a day trip which left about 11 o'clock in the morning. We couldn't wait to get out there. I had never been abroad – we used to go to Blackpool for our holidays – and I'd never been on an aeroplane before either so there was a mixture of nerves and excitement. The plane was full of Rangers fans and we sang all the way over. I never really saw much of Barcelona. We got bussed from the airport into the centre of the city with the travel rep pointing places out saying, This is this place, and this is that place, but we weren't interested, we just wanted to go to the game. The atmosphere before we went out to the stadium was brilliant, all the supporters were in the bars and on the streets. It was so different from the games I'd been to before. You were in a different country and your team was in the final of a European competition.'[21]

Rangers were at a clear advantage given the fact that there were no Russian supporters backing their team in Spain. Sergei Markov explains, 'To say that we were not allowed to go to Barcelona to see the match is not right. It was not a question of allowance – it was a question of practice and life. At that time it was impossible to go abroad any time you wished. Normally it took 2-3 months to pass all the commissions (Communist Party), to fill in all the questionnaires, be checked by the KGB and receive your travel documents to go abroad. So no such thing as a visit to the next match in the European tournament was possible. It was an existing order, so there was no point in being upset about that. Though certainly now we see how improper and inhuman such an order was. I can only wish that my children and grandchildren will learn about that only from history books and not experience. But at that time there was no great sorrow. We understood that if such a final were in Moscow for example, very few Scottish fans could have visited our country.'[22]

Nonetheless, despite their absence from the game, the Russians were as equally passionate as the Rangers fans. Ded Borzov recalls, 'The game was a big event in Moscow. My boss had erected a big television screen and about fifty people crammed in the laboratory, mostly Spartak and CSKA supporters. Everywhere flew a spirit of the imminent victory.'[23]

Sergei Markov says, 'I watched the match on TV at home. Again in those times there were no fans' clubs or pubs with TV-sets where nowadays people gather to watch such matches. Sometimes we gathered together, two, three or four of us at somebody's place. But this time it was a Wednesday and rather late, so I was alone.'[24]

Stay-at-home Rangers fans weren't so

lucky with regards television coverage. There were around thirty countries taking the game live but Scotland wasn't one of them. The national team were playing Wales at Hampden in the Home Internationals on the same night and the SFA wouldn't allow the game to be broadcast live.

Commentator Archie McPherson recalls, 'Up until relatively recently there was a UEFA charter which said if there was a significant game being played, then you couldn't do a live game on TV in the same country. And of course the SFA would claim Stranraer versus Berwick was significant. So, there were doubts over whether BBC would cover the game. They were saying if they can't do the game live they weren't going to do the game at all. There was an internal debate about it and eventually objections were overcome. At the end of the game they simply rewound the tape and played it.'[25]

The local Catalans never really took the game to heart, perhaps because they could see it live on television and consequently there was a poor turnout of neutrals. Jordi Robisoro was one of the few Spanish fans who did turn up. He recalls, 'My grandfather got two tickets, one for me and one for my friend. He was a member of the staff at Barcelona and I went every Sunday to see them and I was a *socio*, an affiliate of the club. I was supporting Glasgow Rangers and my memory is of very kind people. We were young, impressed and amazed by the support. Before the game the fans were very happy and excited. The local people supported Rangers because the Scottish and the Catalans are similar peoples, they have the same mentality. I know now that Rangers are Protestant and Celtic are Catholic but we didn't care about that. We were very quick to get away after the game so I didn't see what they did inside the stadium. I saw people happy and excited and drunk but it was nothing bad. And for many years later I used to wear a blue Rangers rosette, one that a supporter gave me.'[26]

The Russians, all twenty four of them, who had secreted themselves away during the build-up, had their eyes opened in the hours leading up to the match. The great Lev Yashin, a Dynamo coach, recalled the scenes before the game: 'In the Barcelona streets we saw a lot of buses and cars with Scottish fans. With tousled hair, partially naked, obviously boozed from the early morning they shouted, sang and screamed for Rangers, hung banners calling the locals to sympathise with the Scottish club. If you add to that the exotic headwear of the fans – cylinder hats with Rangers crests, mottle bands, big pictures of the players stuck to breasts or backs, drums, horns, Scottish bagpipes – you will get a general picture of the city centre before the match.'[27]

Colin Stein recalls the Scottish team's trip from the secluded hotel to the ground, 'I remember going up to the stadium and it was quiet and then

Barcelona – here we come!

Jock Wallace,
Willie Waddell
and Stan
Anderson
*work out a
plan in
Barcelona*

all of a sudden it was a sea of red, white and blue all around us. The fans started banging on the side of the bus and it was vibrating. It was a great atmosphere.'[28]

Archie McPherson, the BBC commentator on that night recalls, 'It was bizarre. When we got to the stadium, very early, there were Rangers fans walking all over the pitch, not doing any harm, just walking around. There was no security whatsoever and we thought then, Oh, this could be difficult.'[29]

Despite Rangers' poor end to the season there were few real dilemmas over the team selection. Greig, despite not playing in the league since April 10th against Dundee, had made a couple of substitute appearances in the friendly games before the final and would play – fit or not! It was a huge risk and Colin Stein says, 'None of the players knew just how badly John was injured. He was an inspiration but I think if the players had known how bad he was we would have thought twice about it because what if he had let us down? So it was definitely a gamble.'[30]

But Alex MacDonald said, 'You never wanted him out of the team even if he was half-fit. He had such presence.'[31]

Colin Jackson, a certain starter, got injured just prior to the game, forcing a late team re-shuffle. Alex MacDonald recalls the Jackson blow, 'The saddest thing about the game is the injury to big Colin. It must have been horrendous for him. We were playing 5-a-sides behind the goal and he went over on his ankle. It went up like a balloon. It was a shame. I've never even asked him about it, I've only started to talk about it now, thirty years on. Big Colin has never said a word about it. It's typical of him though, he's such a big gentleman.'[32]

The unlucky Jackson remembers that fateful day all too well. He said, 'We'd had a team talk and been told how we'd play and went out for a kick-about. There was a rut in the ground and the ball went past me, I turned and my ankle disappeared in the rut. I went down in a heap and I knew right away it was bad. I tried to get up but couldn't. Within ten minutes it had ballooned up and I knew it was over for me. There was nothing we could do for it. I was shattered. The boys were sympathetic but I just wanted to sit in the corner myself.

'On the day of the match I was with Ronnie McKinnon, and the rest of the boys were going up at 1 o'clock in the afternoon for a rest. Ronnie said, Why don't we get a jug of sangria? So we drank that and then went up to the room at about 2 o'clock. Ronnie then got out the cigars and produced a bottle of Harvey's Bristol Cream in a big dark blue bottle. Then the old masseur Tam Paterson knocked on the door to see if we were okay. He disappeared and came back with a bottle of gin! Tam had a couple of drinks and then left Ronnie and I to it. Big Jock came to the room about 4.30 just before the pre-match meal and had to fight his way through the smoke and fumes. He grabbed me and threw me in the shower, calling me all the names under the sun. He's shouting, You stupid bastard, what if there's a replay? and I'm saying, Don't worry, we'll beat them, we'll win it. He turned the shower on and I still had my clothes on. So I stood there getting drenched but it sobered me up a bit. Nobody said too much though because they knew the situation.

'When we got to the stadium before the game I was taking in the atmosphere and that was the worst time, that's when it got to me. I went away and sat in the dug-out myself for ten minutes. At that time, with the combination of the drink and what have you I was feeling a bit morose and I was close to tears. It was big Jock who came out and dragged me back into the dressing room, he was really good about it. In fact when I left the dressing room to go up to the stand I was almost relieved to let them get on with it.

'It was fate, just one of these things and since that night I've just got on with it. It happens to a lot of other players. I was fortunate that I never had any serious injuries so I had a reasonably long career. I won a few Scotland caps which made up for it. You see the pictures of that night and remember that you were so close to playing. But there were 13 medals and big Ronnie and I got the other two so they can't take that away from me.'[33]

With Derek Johnstone dropping into the centre half position there was a midfield berth up for grabs with Andy Penman, Derek Parlane and Alfie Conn all in contention. Bobby Maitland of the *Evening Citizen* told readers that, 'Waddell called the player (Penman) in from the Spanish sun and told him he would be playing.'[34] In the event, it was Alfie Conn who got the nod!

Rangers' desperation to win permeated the club, fans and players. Willie Johnston said, 'We were confident but there was such pressure on us to win. With Celtic winning the European Cup in 1967 and us losing two European finals there was a lot of pressure on. Those of us who had played in Nuremberg in 1967 felt it worse, we didn't want to let the fans down again. I was hoping on the night that we'd have a good game but I would have taken anything to win, even an own goal.'[35]

Pre-match instructions for both teams were significantly different and, as it turned out, had a major bearing on the outcome. Waddell's plans had been basic. Johnston recalls, 'A few nights before the game we had a team talk and Waddell talked to us about the Russians. They were very strong and technically excellent. Sabo was their playmaker and Greig was told, nail him, an instruction which to be honest, is something that happens in every game.'[36]

The Russians were less decisive and their inexperience on the European stage clearly affected them. Goalkeeper Pilguy said, 'In Moscow before our departure we were given a big talk. Ivonin, Deputy Chairman of the USSR sport committee, considered we needed a grand speech to boost morale. We didn't need it, we knew we were playing for the honour of Soviet football.'[37]

Captain Valery Zykov remembers the confusion in the Dynamo camp. 'I think our coaches were mistaken in their plans. They should not have changed our sharp attacking game which our team played brilliantly. Three times we were summoned by them and told three different game plans! The final plan, confident defence and quick counter attacks did not work and only when we were 3-0 down did we change it.'[38]

Rangers 3 Moscow Dynamo 2

Nou Camp, Barcelona, 24th May 1972

Both sides were similarly handicapped in playing terms. Rangers had two players missing through injury, Jackson and McKinnon and the Ibrox men lined up: McCloy, Jardine, Mathieson, Greig (Captain), Derek Johnstone, Smith, McLean, Conn, Stein, MacDonald, Willie Johnston. (scorers – Stein 24, Johnston 40, 49)

Dynamo also had two players out, their influential strikers Vladimir Koslov and Anatoly Kozhenyakin. The Russians lined up: Pilguy, Basalaev, Dolmatov, Zykov (Captain), Dolbonosov (Gershkovich, 68), Zhukov, Baydachny, Yakubik (Eshtrekov, 57), Sabo, Makhovikov, Evryuzhikhin. (scorers – Eshtrekov 59, Makhovikov 87)

The scene was set for a night of unforgettable drama. The Rangers players had been confined to their hotel for the best part of three days, growing ever more pensive and anxious. It hadn't helped that neither team was allowed to warm up on the pitch before the game. As they emerged from the underground dressing rooms the Scots looked wound-up and ready to explode their pent-up energy. Greig looked confident, a born leader of men. MacDonald's nervous agitation had him swinging his arms to loosen up, ready for battle to commence.

The explosion from the stands at the sight of the blue jerseys was deafening, a cacophony of noise and colour that had been stored up and carried around by the Ibrox support since 1967. The cheering, shouting and almost frenzied encouragement of the Rangers fans immediately manifested itself in two different ways. It served to increase the pressure on the Ibrox players – they simply daren't lose. However, on the plus side, their Russian opponents discovered a new level of loneliness. The pensive, ordered Dynamo players, with their contrasting soldier-like short back and sides, looked as if the Nou Camp was the last place on earth they wanted to be.

After the pre-match formalities Rangers broke away to the left of the tunnel with an energy and zeal which would see them stamp their authority over the early stages of the game. Captain Greig, with little thought of protecting his injury, carried out Waddell's instructions to the letter. The first five seconds illustrates perfectly one important change in the game since the seventies. That's all it took for Greig to slide into Sabo from behind letting the talented midfielder know 'he was in a game'. To his credit, the Russian never exaggerated his obvious pain, instead, restricting himself to a withering look of disdain at Greig. (In fact the lack of play-acting was a refreshing feature of a final where a few late tackles were going in.)

Nowadays, however, Greig's 'message' would almost certainly have resulted in a yellow card which would have curtailed the Rangers skipper's effectiveness for the rest of the 90 minutes. As it was, he escaped a caution and for the rest of the game threw himself into challenges, inspiring his team mates who responded magnificently.

The Ibrox men's work-rate, team spirit, energy and application was immense. There was an inspirational honesty about the Scots' performance typified by Colin Stein, for whom the word rampage was surely invented. It was the ex-Hibs player's finale to a great personal campaign and he fought as if his life depended on it.

The first half saw Rangers play with aggression and no little skill although the Russians looked dangerous on the break. There was little between the teams and Stein admits, 'A lot of people thought we were away ahead of them in the first half but that wasn't true. It was very tight. They weren't any worse than us, that's for sure.'[39] Dave Smith and Derek Johnstone, an unlikely centre

Rangers 3 Moscow Dynamo 2

Jardine and Johnstone challenge with two Russians in the final

back duo, were steady, showing some nice touches in control although, unsurprisingly, gaps occasionally opened up.

The Russians should have taken the lead when Baydachny beat Mathieson on the byeline and cut the ball back to the edge of the six yard box where it found Yakubik. With the whole gaping goal to aim at and McCloy stranded, the Russian somehow contrived to skew his shot wide of the post. It was a glorious chance and one which could have changed the course of the game. It was a let-off the Ibrox side would soon capitalise on.

Rangers were by far the more aggressive and had more than their fair share of possession but the Russians continued to look dangerous and several defence-splitting passes from the midfield carried just too much weight to cause any real problems for the Ibrox defence. Dynamo continued to probe sporadically and a speculative 30-yard shot from Makhovikov had Peter McCloy grasping at the ball gladly at the second attempt.

It was Tommy McLean however, who boosted the Scots when he had their first attempt on goal, cutting in and shooting from the edge of the box. It was an effort which never really troubled Pilguy in the Dynamo goal but it served to raise the energy levels of the Ibrox players and fans who seemed to feed off each other as confidence grew.

Dave Smith, Scotland's Player of the Year that season, had his finest hour. The Aberdonian showed all his class in the final and his mazy run might have resulted in Rangers' first goal. Smith cruised past three Russians on his way to the edge of the box before setting up Alex MacDonald but the little midfielder's first touch let him down and the chance was lost. The game was heating up nicely.

There seemed no real danger for the Russians in the 24th minute when Rangers scored their first goal. Jardine should have been penalised for a tackle on the touchline, but as everyone hesitated, the referee Ortiz de Mendebil played on and the loose ball arrived at the feet of Dave Smith. Stein takes up the story, 'I started running and Dave picked me out. I ran through with the centre half close to me and whacked it into the top corner of the net. I got it on the half volley and really smacked it. I turned away to celebrate and there was nothing but Rangers fans on the park.' [40]

Willie Johnston adds, 'It was a brilliant goal. Stein was brilliant away from home because he was a workhorse. He would have a go from anywhere and it was a great strike.'[41]

The Russian perspective on the crucial opening goal is unsurprisingly different. Zykov claimed, 'Their first goal was scored after an obvious referee's fault. He did not react to a foul by Rangers defender Jardine against Alexander Makhovikov and as a result the ball went to Smith who

Barcelona – here we come!

passed it brilliantly to Stein in our penalty area. Stein was only passively covered by Dolmatov, probably because our defender could not believe that the referee would not react to an obvious foul. So Dolmatov missed the moment when Stein accelerated.'[42]

The Russians looked shell-shocked as Rangers' harrying and chasing continued unabated. Alex MacDonald and John Greig put in endless tackles to break up the Russians' rhythm. All this was set against a shrill background of whistle and horns, giving the game a real continental feel. But the Russians remained slick on the break and only a good close-range block from McCloy prevented Dynamo drawing level. However, with only five minutes remaining in the first half Rangers doubled their lead with a simple goal.

Smith was again the architect, picking the ball up just inside the Rangers half and taking it on a run in the inside right channel. Under pressure he checked, turned inside and swung over a cross into the goalmouth. Johnston remembers, 'I came in from the wing and when Davie pulled it onto his left foot I knew where the ball was going. He'd done that often enough, so that's where I used to make my runs. I wasn't bad in the air and if I got a run on a player I could get up. I knew where I was putting it, just a glance to knock into the corner.'[43]

However, there were more ominous signs as the low level cameras panned to Stein ushering celebrating fans off the pitch. Rangers' confidence was at its peak and Derek Johnstone pushed up to try his luck from outside the box only to see the ball fly high over the bar. On the half-time whistle the almost disbelieving fans let out a thunderous roar knowing that only a second half collapse could rob them of victory. Some got a bit carried away and one Spanish onlooker noted one fan displaying, 'unbelievable passion, foaming at the mouth, half naked, with mad eyes bulging – nobody dared say anything bad about Rangers.'[44]

More sober fans might have noticed that Rangers had changed their shirts at half-time. Alex MacDonald explained, 'We wanted to keep the shirts we started the game with because they had a special commemorative badge. So we put on another set of shirts so we could swap them after the game. The ones we had on in the first half were soaked with sweat but the ones we changed into were even heavier! A few weeks before the final we had seen new, special lightweight shirts in the dressing room but Waddell had said they weren't the right colour of blue so he sent them back!'[45]

The Ibrox men's grip on the Cup was strengthened only four minutes after the break when Rangers scored a third goal in what is now described in the game, usually in a critical way, as 'route one' football. McCloy's long punt up the field is tracked by the television camera going high up into the night sky, against the backdrop of the steep

Nou Camp slopes and the eye is inevitably drawn to the ball's flight path. It eventually landed at a seemingly offside Willie Johnston who shows good composure to drive it low past the Russian keeper.

The ball was so long in the air it is impossible to judge the offside situation but Johnston remains adamant, saying, 'I definitely wasn't offside for my second goal. Peter used to tell me he'd launch into the inside forward positions. I'd go along in front of the defence and then make my run. That's what happened at that goal. The Russians tried to play me offside but I was giving them five yards of a start. I knew I wasn't offside and I knew I had plenty of time. I could have taken it in a bit further but I decided to hit it quickly because the keeper wasn't ready.'[46]

Unsurprisingly the Dynamo camp remains equally dogmatic, captain Zykov saying, 'He was obviously offside.'[47]

The Rangers players or fans weren't too concerned when Dynamo pulled one back in the 59th minute through substitute Eshtrekov who had been on the park only three minutes. It was a goal that needn't have been given away. Evryuzhikhin cut out Mathieson's sloppy pass back to Jardine at the edge of the Rangers box (two full backs on the same side of the pitch!). He slipped the ball past the onrushing McCloy to the speeding Eshtrekov, who looked offside, and the Russian knocked the ball into the empty goal. However, with half an hour to play even the Russian

players didn't think a comeback was on the cards. The Dynamo substitute admitted, 'I was less enthusaistic about my goal than I was about the second by Sasha Makhovikov.'[48]

But gradually the Dynamo players sensed that they could claw back the two goals needed and as the second half wore on the ball was increasingly drawn towards the Rangers goal. McCloy had to make several important saves and Smith and Jardine both made crucial interceptions although Stein came close at the other end. It seemed that Rangers had hung on but four minutes from the end they conceded the second goal, thus setting up a barnstorming finale. Sasha Makhovikov took a pass from Gershkovich, dribbled through a tired Rangers defence and despite falling to the ground crashed a shot past McCloy high into the net.

The fans began to panic and Billy McMahon recalled, 'Rangers were outstanding in the first half but we could see they were getting tired with the heat and the effort they had put into the game. If the game had gone another five or ten minutes they would have been caught. With minutes to go the referee gave a throw-in to Rangers in at the corner and gave one long blast of the whistle and the crowd thought the game was finished so they came on. They got them off the park but they stood on the touchlines. I was only thirty at the time but the older fans were screaming at the Rangers fans to get off the pitch.'[49]

Johnston scoring Rangers' second goal

Archie McPherson recalls, 'The last twenty minutes of the game were astonishing. We were in a terrible viewing position, down at pitch level. We were sitting amongst the supporters and there was one supporter virtually sitting on my knee with a bottle of Pundador and he was trying to give me a drink. They thought the game was won at that time.'[50]

Jordi Rosiboro said, 'I remember it was good for Rangers, one nil, two nil, then three nil, but finally the Russians came back. Dynamo Moscow were very good and in the final moments I wanted them to equalise so the game could go to extra time.'[51]

Colin Glass recalls, 'I was out in the garden with a few mates listening on this big blue radio to the great David Francey's commentary. But I remember that when I watched it on television

later, we weren't nearly in as in much danger in the second half as Francey had made out.'[52]

Ded Borzov remembered, 'Curses and strong words were heard in our laboratory. I've never heard so many bad words about Dynamo in all my life. But it was quite understandable because a sure feast was spoiled.'[53]

Jack Bain remembers, 'We were up in the second tier and with a couple of minutes to go we started to make our way down to the pitch side. We wanted to go on the park like the Celtic fans did in Lisbon.'[54]

The final whistle, when it did come, heralded an almost comical pitch invasion. Like greyhounds out of the traps the fans bolted onto the field.

Colin Stein says, 'I was in the centre circle and I was off, away down the steps to the dressing room before all the fans got on. I was waiting for the other players to come down. The fans were trying to get down with us but they were being stopped. In hindsight if the police had left them it would have been alright.'[55]

Peter McCloy recalls, 'I'd no chance of getting from the goals to the tunnel. I was going down under the heap of fans who were ecstatic and didn't realise they were in danger of crushing me. Luckily there were two or three sober fans who lifted me right up on their shoulders and carried me off the park. If the authorities had just let them run daft for five minutes and then made an announcement for them to get off it would have been fine.'[56]

Tommy McLean says, 'It was quite scary because I was gasping for air and with me not being the tallest I was lost amongst it all.'[57]

Sandy Jardine recalls, 'It was a struggle to get off the park. The fans were exuberant but didn't realise what they were doing to us, pulling us and pushing us. We didn't know what was going on upstairs. We thought they were just going to clear the pitch and we'd go up and get the trophy. We were tired and absolutely overjoyed so we didn't realise the full extent of the problems.'[58]

Eventually, the players made it into the dressing room and it became clear the situation was beyond control. With proper security and a public address system it would have taken little to clear the pitch and get a proper presentation. But the UEFA officials weren't prepared to wait and instead John Greig and Willie Waddell were taken through a labyrinth of corridors and handed the Cup. Being denied the symbolism of picking up the European trophy in public was the single most disappointing aspect of the whole campaign, for Greig and the fans.

Greig recalled, 'One of the officials handed the trophy to me with hardly a word and then we were back on our way to the dressing room. Waddell was absolutely raging, he was totally disgusted at the manner in which the trophy was presented. It was one of the greatest nights of my career but in the end it was a real slap in the face for Rangers.'[59]

Archie McPherson says, 'John Greig came down and was talking to the press in a fairly agitated state. There was no exultation but to be honest Billy McNeil was the same in Lisbon. They were just so overcome with events there was almost an anti-climax to it.'[60]

That sense of anti-climax is not often linked with Lisbon '67 in the same way as it has been with Barcelona '72. But Lisbon Lion Jim Craig recalled a similar sense of disappointment at the end of the European Cup final. Talking about the Celtic fans on that famous night he praised them but added, 'Their actions took a little of the gloss off the proceedings for me. It would have been wonderful to do a lap of honour, not just for the fans present in Lisbon but for the many thousands of others watching on television. The presentation of our medals was anti-climactic to say the least. After being kept waiting for a long time by the Italians at the ensuing banquet, an offical came up and placed two containers of medals on our table. We more or less helped ourselves.'[61]

Back in Scotland the stay-at-home fans endured their own stresses and strains. Garry Lynch said, 'I was only fifteen at the time and wasn't allowed to go. As it was a delayed transmission I didn't want to know the score. So I went to Hampden to see Scotland v Wales. It was bizarre when you think of it, imagine Scotland playing when a Scottish club side is in the final of a European competition. I must have been the only Rangers fan at the game, there was certainly no talk around me on the terracing about how they were getting on. Afterwards I quickly got the train back to Kirkhill, walked along to the chip shop and someone said, That was some score for Rangers tonight! So I knew they had won. I was elated and floated all the way along the road. I got back in time to watch it on the television. And thank Christ I did know the score because I think I would have had a heart attack at the end!'[62]

As the Rangers players and the stay-at-home fans celebrated, up on the pitch things were taking a turn for the worse.

Willie Johnston scores what proves to be Rangers' winning goal

Jubilant Rangers fans invade the pitch at the final whistle.
Note the unmolested and apparently unconcerned Dynamo
defender Basalaev, no 2

Barcelona – here we come!

'MADNESS BREAKS OUT'

A Spanish policeman tries to contain the fans after the final whislte

Barcelona – here we come!

'the only real surprise is that people were surprised'

Since the beginning of football there have been countless harmless pitch invasions following Cup finals and other important matches. Indeed it still happens at home and abroad on a regular basis. Why the Spanish police chose this occasion to instigate a needless battle will never be fully understood. But the fact remains that they did. When the fans stampeded on, the police, who had been friendly enough up to that point, went into riot mode.

The initial euphoria and joy of the fans was replaced by 'fight or flight' self-preservation instincts. As battle commenced, in a random sort of way, there were more than a few Scots who were ready and willing to take the former option. There is little doubt however, that the police were the instigators of the trouble at the stadium and it could have easily been avoided (although the trouble away from the game was solely the fault of the Rangers supporters).

Given the political climate and the previous warnings, the only real surprise was that people were surprised. The potent mix of an overtly aggressive police force and a volatile, widely inebriated mass of working class Scotsmen was a marriage made for the battlefield.

Jordi Rosiboro explained, 'You have to understand what Catalonia was like at that time. Franco was never popular in Barcelona and his police were very aggressive. The locals did not like them at all. You could not talk or gather in the street or they would appear very quickly and disperse everyone. It was normal for the police to have batons and to use them. They would be aggressive and even kill if need be – no problem to them. Arguably, the occasion and the clash with the Scottish people gave them an opportunity to show this aggression.'[1]

Supporter Jack Bain recalls, 'When the police had circled the part of the stadium we were at, I asked one of them if they would let me on. He stood back and let me through. I then heard a whistle and the police turned on the fans and the one who had let me past then hit me across the back with his baton. We tried to get off the other side of the pitch but the fans who had been first off the park turned and started throwing things at the police. It was madness.'[2]

Daily Express photographer Tom McLaren was working at the game and claimed, 'Personally, I think the Spanish police lost it. I moved up to take close-up pictures. . . two of them attacked me.'[3]

Bobby Brown ex-Rangers keeper and former Scotland team boss was present and his recollection was of two Spanish policemen holding a young fan whilst another colleague beat him up.[4]

One unnamed British resident claimed in the next morning's *Daily Express*, 'The fans were rowdy, noisy and drunk in a carnival way until they were provoked by the police with the usual flailing batons. My Spanish friends were apologising to me for the police handling of the boisterous crowd. . . the Spanish television cameras as usual were moved off the incidents to quieter sections of the crowd.'[5]

Commentator Archie McPherson recalled, 'The police were out of order. They were very heavy-handed. I'm not trying to minimise what the Rangers fans did but I remember standing with the Reuters correspondent and he said, "Look down there, that's the fascist police in action. They don't know how to control a crowd, they only know one way and that's to lash out." On a click the police turned round and started to clobber the Rangers supporters. And when the trouble started the Spanish cameraman panned away from it. So we were trying to describe the scenes on the pitch and he had turned to the right and was showing the traffic in the streets outside!'[6]

Trying to negotiate their way back safely to their transport and hotels, rather than see their heroes with the trophy, became the main concern of the fans.

Billy McMahon recalled, 'When we made our way back to the buses the police were trying to extort money from us. My friend and I were stopped outside the stadium by this policeman who demanded we hand over our pesetas. My friend said no, so the policeman swung his gun at him, missed him but got me on the back of the knee. We saw one woman with a Rangers scarf on lying in the bushes. The police had battered her and there was blood everywhere, coming out of her ears, everywhere. There was no trouble in our hotel when we got back but when we went for a walk in the town we saw plenty of bother. We walked into a hotel called the El Presidente and it was deadly quiet. We asked another Rangers fan what was going on and he said, "I think the first person that moves is getting shot!" The police were standing with guns. The next day we went to a barbecue organised by the hotel and the police were still there, looking at us in a non too friendly way.'[7]

Jack Bain had a similar experience, 'I got separated from my friends and had to make my own way out of the stadium. I was sure I was going to be attacked by the police but luckily I got away. We got back to our hotel and were glad to see our bar was still open. I remember looking up and there was a machine gun set up on a coffee table and it was facing us!'[8]

John Miller added, 'If you had a scarf on that night you were in trouble. Remember the Provvy man, who gave me the money to go? Well, he must have been about 60 at the time but he

got caught up in it all. When he came to my house the following week he was still black and blue.'[9]

John Powell recalls, 'The night was fraught with danger as police were picking people up at random. We made our way back to the Ramblas and what should have been a night of celebration turned out to be an anti-climax. Next morning saw a change of attitude amongst the Barcelona people. Twenty four hours previously these people had enjoyed our company but now treated us with contempt. We had to leave our accommodation before 12 noon or the owner threatened to keep our passports. Whilst in a bar having some food we had a visit from "Franco's Henchmen" who poured over us and removed a steel comb from a mate's pocket, bent it in front of him, and threw it along the floor. The whole experience was quite scary. We thought we had seen the back of them but on leaving the cafe, a car pulled up – I don't know if it was the same crew – and the police grabbed my friend who was dressed in a kilt and drove off. I honestly thought I would never see him again. We took the Metro to the main station and about ten minutes before we left my mate arrived slightly bruised, shaken, but still in good spirits. The journey home was so welcome with so many looking forward to seeing Glasgow Central. But me, I was happy when I saw the white cliffs of Dover.'[10]

Rangers Football Club as an institution no longer had the inherent and tradit-

Rangers' victorious squad rest at their hotel and admire the trophy before returning to Glasgow (l to r) Conn, Johnstone, Parlane, MacDonald, Jardine, Jackson, McCloy, McKinnon, Miller

ional backing of the Scottish press and they suffered accordingly. The immediate verdict was that the travelling fans were guilty.[11]

The front page of the *Daily Express* screamed, Battle of Barcelona and stated that, 'thousands of Rangers fans disgracefully marred the teams magnificent victory.'[12] The *Daily Record* cried, Victory and Violence from its front page with journalist Alex Cameron writing, 'I have reported in most parts of the world in the last twenty five years but I can honestly say I have never seen anything as unruly and stupid anywhere.'[13]

Allan Herron, after a few days in which to reflect, savaged the Rangers fans in a *Sunday Mail* article headed, Ibrox Guttersnipes. He wrote, 'Let there be no excuses. The fans were to blame for what happened in Barcelona.' Perhaps he had more of a point when he asked, 'What provoked the fans into wrecking hotels, throwing bottles from hotel balconies, smashing cars, tearing restaurants and floral displays apart?'[14]

The *Glasgow Herald* was inevitably outraged and introduced a broader perspective to the debate. In its editorial, it asked, in all seriousness, 'How many investors might think twice before choosing to set up in Scotland?'[15] The almost stereotypical 'outraged of Bearsden' was moved to write in and offer their tuppenceworth. A certain CK McLean, also widening the issue, asked, 'What was the cost of the trip and how many of the fans have been on strike for higher wages since the year began? With regards to the "right to work", do these not exclude the right to down tools to attend midweek sports meetings.'[16]

Given the political strength of Franco's dictatorial regime, there was no surprise that the Spanish press were totally antagonistic towards the Scots. In terms of the game itself, *El Noticeria* said it was 'devoid of the greatest beauties of football, or at least what Spain regards as good football.'[17]

El Correa's headline, Sad Final – Unprecedented Sadness, encapsulated the feeling of the time. Reporter Morera Falco was critical of the Scottish fans claiming that their invasion of Barcelona beforehand had set the scene for the team's victory and added, 'With the fans constantly singing and shouting throughout the whole game the only outcome was a Scottish victory. It wasn't their football which won but the fans.'[18]

It was open season on the Scots and the following day journalist Lorenzo Contreras from the Madrid newspaper *Cronica Madrid* said, 'Perhaps the Glasgow fans thought that their behaviour was valid because they were confusing our country with some old British colony like Kenya or Bengal.'[19] However, arguably more worrying was the report that as a result of their part in the trouble after the game, the police had sent three Rangers fans to a local psychiatric unit![20]

El Correa reported on Operation Return as arrangements were made by the Spanish authorities to get all the fans back to Scotland. [21] Fans were put in vans and sent to the airport regardless of destination or indeed whether they had come by aeroplane at all.

Billy McMahon says, 'When we got to Barcelona airport on the Friday to go home they were putting us on any flight. We finished up coming into Prestwick instead of Glasgow. It was ridiculous. When we arrived we found that some fans had had their cases ransacked and their duty-free stolen.' [22]

Instead of savouring their first European trophy the Ibrox club and its followers were under attack. But despite the unfairness of what happened inside the ground, and strong evidence pointed to police over-reaction, there was an element of hooliganism amongst the Rangers fans which cannot be denied. Photographs in the newspapers in the following days showed the damage done to the stadium and part of the town, seats broken, broken windows, plant pots smashed and there was genuine shock that the Scots would repay the hospitality of their hosts with this sort of behaviour. [23]

There was also plenty of in-house criticism and in hindsight it appears admirably forthright and almost incredible in its intensity. Willie Waddell made several references to the unruly element of the Rangers support that night in Spain but saved his most scathing attack for the beginning of the new season when in 'a declaration of war' against 'the unruly mob who spread destruction and venom' he was quoted in a newspaper article as saying, 'It's to these tikes, hooligans, louts and drunkards that I pinpoint my message. It is because of your gutter rat behaviour that we are being publicly tarred and feathered.' [24] The secretary of the Rangers Supporters Association, Duncan Perret was also critical of his fellow fans saying, 'I am sick to the teeth of some of our support. These people never seem to learn a lesson.' [25]

Moscow Dynamo had put in a formal protest immediately after the match and the repercussions were up for debate. Lev Yashin said, 'In numerous press interviews Konstantine Beskov and me explained all our dissatisfaction and displeasure with the surroundings of the match. According to the rules we sent a telegram to UEFA in Bern confirming our protest.' [26] The Russians had some heavyweight support from Gustav Widerker, the UEFA President who said, 'The behaviour of the Scottish fans was appalling and disgusting. I support the Dynamo protest, but the question of a replay may be finally decided on at the UEFA sitting.' [27]

Dynamo scorer Vladimir Eshtrekov recalls, 'Most of the fans were drunk. It was obviously something new for Barcelona, and the police were helpless. We filed a protest and were ready to replay the match anywhere and whenever, but the decision was to award the cup to Glasgow Rangers. And we Russians say that our teams have been treated unfairly only recently!'[28]

Dynamo captain Valery Zykov, in reminiscing mood said, 'Every time something reminds me of the game, my mood goes down, as if somebody steps on my sore toe. I am always about to answer with the words of a popular Russian hit song by composer Dobrynin, Do not pour salt on my wound, it's still not healed. Indeed, that match is forever left in its particip- ants' minds – for some as a long-wished victory, for others, as a bitter disillusion because of a victory escaped. Now we almost got used to fans interrupting matches, various incidents including fatal tragedies that happened at football matches in the '80s and '90s, when vandalism and hooliganism of football fans became nearly an ordinary thing, taught us not to be surprised of match interruptions. But then masses of fans pouring onto the pitch, most of them warmed with drinks that were far from being soft, became a real shock for everybody – players, UEFA officials, journalists.' [29]

A UEFA spokesman declared that the Discipline Committee of UEFA would gather at an extraordinary meeting in order to discuss Dynamo's protest. [30]

Despite UEFA's notoriety for bizarre decisions Rangers were unconcerned about the possibility of the trophy being taken back. The Ibrox party flew back to Scotland the next day and were met by Glasgow's Lord Provost John Mains with rivals Celtic represented by director Desmond White – repaying Rangers' gesture after Lisbon. Mains, who had not been in Barcelona, later described the behaviour of the Rangers fans as 'shameful and disgraceful'. However, when asked about the activities of the Spanish police he said, 'I would not want to criticise because I wasn't there!'[31]

The Rangers squad made their way over to Ibrox to show off the coveted silverware to the fans. It made for an odd occasion. The rain lashed down as the tracksuited Rangers players boarded what looked like a coal lorry that had been adorned by a bedraggled Union flag.

Colin Glass remembers, 'I arrived at lunchtime and there were some kids on the roof of Bellahouston Primary School dancing and singing with their scarves. When the players did arrive, hours later, the fans were soaked but they sang that song which went, *We've got Peter McCloy, number one* and went through the whole eleven players!'[32]

Although there were many sombrer- os and souvenirs of Barcelona, many of the fans were still in Spain, or making their way home, thus missing the chance to see the team parade the trophy. Those who were on the rain- drenched slopes of Ibrox sang to Greig that they wanted to see his talismanic beard off. Greig however, waited until the next day to become clean shaven once again. It was a strange end to a strange season.

Barcelona – here we come!

Rangers players and management show off the silverware back at Ibrox

*Rangers Captain John Greig with final goalscorers
Willie Johnston and Colin Stein*

Barcelona – here we come!

9
EPILOGUE

The fall-out from Barcelona was suitably chaotic. The gnashing of teeth in Scotland soon subsided but sanctions from abroad hit the Ibrox club hard. After a UEFA disciplinary hearing Rangers found themselves banned from all European competitions for two years, later reduced to one year after the persuasive Waddell had successfully appealed. Instead of being allowed the chance to become the first, and only club to retain the trophy, Rangers had to watch Hibs take their place.

That their official centenary season, 1972/73, was also their first ever as European trophy holders should have been a matter of pride to Rangers FC but their European ban and having their image tarnished across the continent meant that what should have been a glorious afterglow became a tawdry conclusion.

Partly as a result of their exclusion and partly because of their centenary celebrations Rangers invited reigning European Cup holders Ajax to play in a friendly at Ibrox in January 1973. When the Dutchmen arranged a return in Amsterdam a week later, Rangers found they had inadvertently founded the European Super Cup. Europe's governing body eventually sanctioned this play-off between the holders of the Champions Cup and the Cup Winners Cup which subsequently became an annual event now played as a one-off match in Monaco. It is, of course, glib to suggest that when the UEFA junketeers congregate in the South of France each year, they should raise their glasses to the Rangers supporters.

But it would be wrong to think the Super Cup was occupying minds at Ibrox in the aftermath of Barcelona. To add to the Ibrox turmoil, Waddell made headlines of his own only two weeks after returning from Spain by opting out of the manager's seat, leaving Jock Wallace to take over. Although Waddell retained considerable power, it was the end of a short-lived era and Wallace set about building his own side but soon found that times were moving on and he consequently encountered problems of his own.

Wallace's move up from coach came at a time when attitudes amongst Old Firm players were changing. The lure of English gold was proving hard to resist. For decades the Glasgow giants had relied on the old fashioned notion of, 'playing for the jersey', which, allied to the restrictive minimum wage in England, had been powerful enough to prevent most of their best players heading down the A74 to exploit their skills.

But the financial North/South divide was becoming increasingly difficult to ignore. Tales of Southern treasures reached Glasgow often via the Anglos

Barcelona – here we come!

in the Scotland national team, some of whom had by-passed the relative poverty of Scottish football and gone straight to England. Willie Henderson had left to go to Sheffield Wednesday and Rangers' Barcelona goal heroes, Colin Stein and Willie Johnston, soon found their way to the lucrative English First Division.

Willie Johnston found himself at a crossroads, 'I wanted a transfer after that season because of money, £20 per week to be exact. I was signing monthly contracts when Waddell offered me a 6-year contract. He called me into his office, put it in front of me and said, Sign that. I asked what I was getting and he said, £60 per week. I said I want £80 and a £10 grand signing on fee for over the 6 years. He just blanked me and said, Bud, sign the contract. But I said no. I knew the players in England were getting £130 per week. So I signed for West Brom even though I didn't know they were in Birmingham! But when I got back into the Scotland team the first person to phone me was Waddell saying, Bud, I should never have let you go.[1]

Colin Stein left to join Coventry in October, weeks into the new season. He said, 'I thought I'd done enough and it was time for a change. But I came back again and scored the goal at Easter Road to win the league (in 1975). We actually would have won it anyway because we had three or four games left to do it but everyone remembers that as the goal which won

back the title. I was 29 when I came and was only 30 when I finished. I maybe should have played on but where do you go?'[2]

A year later, Alfie Conn also got itchy feet and made the trip South to the bright lights of London and Tottenham Hotspur. It was a footballing trend which was to plague Scottish football for years, and it would still be happening save for the sobering fact that the best Scottish players are no longer deemed good enough for the English Premiership.

Waddell seemed to be struggling to come to terms with the increasing financial demands of the players and even in the afterglow of a European triumph, he couldn't cut loose on the purse strings. Colin Jackson recalls how an unlikely ally came to his aid in his quest for a fair share of the players' European bonus.

He said, 'Waddell offered me a £100 bonus and I told him to stick it up his arse. The boys who played got two grand, which was a lot of money at that time. I thought I was going to get maybe about half that because I had played in every round. Jock Stein stayed close to me and I knew his son-in-law John very well. So I was moaning to him about it and he said, Come down to the house tomorrow, big Stein will be in. So I went down and big Jock said to me, Get back into Ibrox and ask for more, that's a disgrace. So I went back to Waddell and he upped it to £500 just like that.

'Waddell liked the antagonism. If you battled with him you went up in his esteem but if you bowed down to him he would trample all over the top of you. He was good for the club but in any individual basis, and that was usually about money, then he was a nightmare. He never told me about offers from Leeds and then Coventry. I found out about the Coventry one because it had been on the television down there. Waddell denied it and we ended up having a screaming match about it. But shortly after that I got back in the team and I never really got left out again.'[3]

Rangers won the Scottish Cup the next season, 1972/73, with a memorable 3-2 win over Celtic but it would be 1974/75 before the title returned to Ibrox for the first time since 1965. However the team had evolved. In addition to losing Henderson and Johnston (Stein had returned), other players such as Ronnie McKinnon, Dave Smith, Alfie Conn, Andy Penman, Willie Mathieson and Gerry Neef had all either retired or left Ibrox whilst Graham Fyfe and Jim Denny never made the breakthrough into first team regulars.

Derek Johnstone and Derek Parlane came of age although both were to establish themselves as strikers. Quinton Young, Ally Scott, Bobby McKean and goalkeeper Stewart Kennedy, who replaced Peter McCloy for a season, all arrived at Ibrox to enjoy a fair measure of domestic success. Rangers went on to win three league titles, including two 'trebles' in the '70s but without making their mark on the European scene.

A glorious home win over Juventus and an away win in Eindhoven saw the Govan side reach the quarter-finals of the 1978/79 European Cup but, although no-one could foresee how slow the death would be, Scottish football's decline in terms of European credibility was by now terminal. In 1992/93 Rangers qualified for the newly expanded version of the European Cup, the Champions League and on a balmy night in Marseilles, came within one goal of qualifying for the final. That season was only the third time in the twenty one years since Barcelona that the Ibrox side had progressed in Europe after Christmas – and it would be another nine years before it would happen again.

Given the good record of Scottish teams in the formative years of European competitions, the Govan club's Cup Winners Cup success was arguably almost inevitable, and might have been a springboard to further European success. Instead, Barcelona was to be as far as the European trail ever went for the Ibrox men. Fan Colin Glass admits, 'If you had said to me thirty years ago we wouldn't win another European trophy I would have told you to go away!'[4]

Despite periods of domestic supremacy, and notwithstanding the occasional good run, Rangers'

European record since 1971/72 has been poor. When a club has almost three decades of constant access to European football – they only failed to qualify once (1980/81) – then questions have to be asked of such a drought.

All avenues to European success have seemingly been explored. When Rangers teams full of home grown Scottish players failed to make an impact in Europe, Graeme Souness's established English internationalists were seen as the necessary catalyst. When that route failed it was thought that 'superior' foreign players would be the answer and Walter Smith, backed by Rangers' owner David Murray, tempted numerous foreign players from all corners of the globe but European credibility remained elusive.

The next throw of the dice dictated that the Ibrox club appoint a foreign coach in the shape of Dick Advocaat to tutor the foreign players. But again, a European blank was drawn. Over the years, myriad reasons have been propagated to explain the poor Ibrox European record – from injuries, suspensions, the 'three-foreigner rule', loss of late goals, players bought too late to integrate into the team, difficult draws, tiredness – every excuse apart from 'leaves on the line'. All problems which other European clubs, many with less talent and financial backing, have been able to surmount. David Murray has admitted that the club's European record is one of only two failures in his business life.[5] Fortunately for the Ibrox

club, failure abroad was set against a backdrop of unprecedented domestic success. Attention turned to Rangers equalling Celtic's nine Championships in a row and this parochial side show, running in tandem with European failures, whilst appeasing the baser instincts of many Rangers fans, only highlighted how poor Scottish football had become.

Despite the huge amounts of money spent in attracting players, coaches and backroom staff from all over the world, winning the Champions League simply isn't on the agenda anymore. Merely to progress into the second phase of the Champions League, or failing that, remain in the UEFA Cup past Christmas is the new, reduced ambition of Rangers and indeed Celtic. The joyful hysteria which enveloped Rangers players, management and fans when they overcame PSG in December 2001 to progress through to the elusive post-Christmas stage of the UEFA Cup, served only as a reminder of how far expectations have fallen. Rangers, along with all other Scottish clubs, are now European minnows and the annual SPL Old Firm shoot-out only serves to deflect attention from that fact.

As stated at the beginning of this book, winning a European trophy is the highpoint in the history of most clubs – one would think this particularly true of a Scottish club – yet Rangers' 1972 Cup Winners Cup victory remains undoubtedly clouded and by three main issues: Celtic winning the European Cup five years earlier, the crowd trouble in the Nou Camp and the domestic troubles which parenthesised Rangers' European run that season.

Looking at these points in reverse order, it's difficult to imagine that fans would allow one poor league campaign to spoil their enjoyment of a European trophy win, especially when the Ibrox club has gorged on them at all other times, winning 99 Scottish domestic trophies by the first season of the new millennium. However, whilst Greig, McKinnon and Henderson had already been members of a great Rangers team and while many of their team-mates on the Cup Winners Cup run would go on to be part of that successful Rangers side of the mid to late seventies, there was no doubt the domestic disappointment of 71/72 had an impact on perception. As did, of course, the success of Celtic at that time. One can't help feeling that anything which alludes to the period 1966-74, even their own team winning a European trophy, will always have painful associations for Rangers supporters as it was first and foremost a time when Celtic dominated the league and won the European Cup.

Celtic's victory in Lisbon was undoubtedly a great triumph for the Parkhead side and for Scottish football but the intense and often twisted Old Firm rivalry ensures the Ibrox club's European trophy is regarded as a poor second instead of a notable first. To present it as anything else might reek of settling for second-best by Rangers.

The final factor in persuading many Rangers people to sweep Barcelona '72 under the blue carpet was the stigma of crowd trouble. There's little doubt that the Rangers fans invaded the pitch simply to emulate the Celtic supporters in the Estadio Nacional five years earlier. It seems that the Rangers supporters' readiness to defend themselves against the Spanish police that night mitigated against their claims of innocence, and their poor behaviour afterwards didn't help their cause.

If the Rangers fans were harshly treated in the Nou Camp, past acts of genuinely malicious pitch invasion – in particular the 1969 Fairs Cup semi-final at Newcastle's St James's Park – made it difficult for the club to claim its followers had been wronged. Subsequent incidents, such as those at Villa Park in 1976, Fir Park, Motherwell in 1978 and the 1980 Scottish Cup final, make it impossible for history to clear the name of the Scottish support at Barcelona.

Before the Criminal Justice (Scotland) Act of 1980 banned alcohol from this country's grounds, there was no cuddly, loveable 'tartan army' facade to Scottish football fans abroad – they were more feared than even the English hooligans and that dark chapter of history can't be easily erased. However, it was an image which was wrongfully attached to the genuinely well-intentioned overspill of emotion on 24th May 1972.

So much for why the club, and perhaps the country's media, don't exactly revel in memories of Barcelona but it's the opinion of today's football fans which counts most when regarding the European achievement of McCloy, Stein, Johnston *et al.* Winning over the general Scottish public is out of the question. As has been argued elsewhere,[6] over the years, Rangers Football Club and their fans have come to embody a social, political and religious ethos which has seen them increasingly marginalised in Scottish society. Moreover, as the richest and most consistently successful club in the country, especially in recent memory, it's therefore doubtful, to say the least, if fans of other Scottish teams will ever regard an Ibrox achievement with any affection.

Also, it is difficult for the Barcelona team to demand due respect from outside Ibrox if it has been less than forthcoming from those within. For the Rangers support it's long been clear they don't consider their early seventies' favourites the greatest of all Ibrox teams. Perhaps it's only because the club and its supporters still dream the dream of the Champions League that prevents them settling their affections on a trophy which is no longer in existence.

Nevertheless, in the final analysis there can be little doubt that what those eighteen players achieved between the Lorient Stadium, Rennes on 15th September 1971 and the Nou Camp, Barcelona on 24th May 1972, rates as the most momentous achievement in the epic history of Glasgow Rangers Football Club.

In the trophy room

Barcelona – here we come!

NOTES

Introduction

1 In 1966, '67, '68, '69 Rangers finished second in the league and never more than five points behind Celtic (who were on their way to nine titles in a row.) In 1970, whilst retaining second spot, they were twelve points behind Celtic. In '71 they slumped to fourth place and in '72 they were sixteen points behind (this in the era of 2 points for a win) and reached neither the Scottish or League Cup final. They were another three seasons away from reclaiming the league title.

2 On the cover of one of the official club history compilations (*Rangers; The Complete Record* Bob Ferrier & Robert McElroy, Breedon Books 1996), there are half a dozen photographs depicting various Ibrox sides over a 100 year period. None of them are of the team that won in Barcelona. One hardly needs to ask whether this would be the case in similar books from Parkhead or Pittodrie.

3 Celtic's Lisbon Lions subsequently became a cottage industry and were a constant source of comfort and inspiration for the beleaguered Parkhead fans through the club's dark period in the 1990s. Aberdeen's Gothenburg heroes are no less omnipotent at Pittodrie.

4 In addition to Rangers winning the European Cup Winners Cup in 1971/72, Celtic reached the semi-final of the European Cup and Aberdeen, St Johnstone and Dundee all went through to the second round of the UEFA Cup. Since then, with a few notable exceptions, Scottish clubs' records in Europe has been poor.

Season 1971/72

1 Archie MacPherson *Action Replays* Chapman 1991 p54. Also see Esplin's *Down the Copland Road* (Argyll, 2000) where the *Daily Record*'s James Traynor is also critical of the sycophantic nature of sportswriters of that era.

2 *Daily Record* 11/09/71 p12

3 *Daily Record* 11/09/71 p12

4 We should be careful when discussing attendances at football stadia throughout the twentieth century. Research for this book has shown that many figures quoted are at best 'guesstimates' and at worst simply invented. For instance Rangers' away leg against Rennes has been recorded as both 13,000 and 20,000. There are also various attendances recorded for the final in Barcelona.

5 *Daily Record* 11/09/71 p12

6 That Scotland played at Hampden on the same night as Rangers were in Barcelona is one indication that the Ibrox club were no longer the 'Establishment team'. The spurious sobriquet is difficult to define but was originally an Ibrox boast (or often an accusation) that Rangers FC as an institution enjoyed special status in Scottish society. This was the case at one time but certainly not any more. The great irony is that cultural, political, social and religious changes and developments in Scotland over the last thirty years mean that if any club can claim that tag, it is Celtic. The authors are currently researching this phenomenon further.

7 *Daily Record* 17/09/71 p31

8 Interview with Willie Johnston 28/10/01

9 Interview with Alex MacDonald 29/10/01

10 Interview with Colin Stein 28/10/01

11 Interview with Alex MacDonald 29/10/01

12 Interview with Tommy McLean 19/12/01

13 Interview with Alex MacDonald 29/10/01

14 The initial *Rangers News* 04/08/1971

15 Interview with Alex MacDonald 29/10/01

16 Interview with Willie Johnston 28/10/01

The journey begins – Rennes

1 This season saw Rangers' best ever performance in the top European competition and they were within one victory, ironically away at Marseilles, of reaching the final.

2 Interview on 7th September 2001. Rennes have four official supporters' clubs which are allocated portacabins situated only yards from the stadium which are used for meetings before the home games.

3 Rennes' first attempt in 1965 had ended in the first round when they went down 2-0 on aggregate to Czech army side Dukla Prague. But to be fair in the early seventies, with European football only a decade or so old, many teams were making their first appearance in European competitions.

4 *Daily Record* 11/11/1971 p14

5 *Glasgow Herald* 12/09/1971

6 Interview with Sandy Jardine 17/09/01

7 Interview with Billy McMahon 10/10/01

8 *Ouest France* 14/09/1971

9 Interview with Peter McCloy 10/12/01

10 Interview with Sandy Jardine 17/09/01

11 *Daily Record* 16/09/1971 p31

12 Interview with Willie Johnston 28/10/01

13 Interview with Alex MacDonald 29/10/01

14 Quoted in Rennes FC Centenary magazine page 48, *L'Histoire du Stade Rennais, 100 ans en Rouge et Noir* published September 2001

15 *Daily Record* 17/09/1971 p31

16 Ouest France 16/09/1971

17 *Daily Record* 17/09/1971 p31

18 Interview with Peter McCloy 10/12/01

19 *Glasgow Herald* 16/09/1971 p6

20 *Daily Record* 27/09/71 p23

21 *Daily Express* 28/09/1971 p22

22 *Ouest France* 26/09/1971

23 *Glasgow Herald* 27/09/71 p4

24 *Glasgow Herald* 28/09/1971 p4

25 Interview with Alex MacDonald 29/10/01

26 *Daily Record* 29/09/1971 p23. Interesting to see the advert below the Rangers match report – Clydebank Amateurs were looking for a fixture for the 1st October!

27 Interview with Sandy Jardine 17/09/01

28 *Daily Record* 30/09/1971 p24

29 *Daily Record* 30/09/1971 p24

30 *Ouest France* 29/09/1971

31 *Evening Times* 29/09/1971 p27

Sporting Lisbon

1 *Daily Express* 2/10/1971 p 20

2 *Daily Express* 5/10/1971, p19

3 *Daily Record*, 18/10/1971 p22

4 *Glasgow Herald* 18/10/1971 p4

5 *A Bola* 1/10/1971

6 *A Bola* 18/10/1971

7 *A Bola* 16/10/1971

8 Interview with Sandy Jardine 17/09/01

9 *Daily Record* 13/10/1971 p25

10 See Esplin's *Down the Copland Road* (Argyll 2000) for a discussion on how the relationship between the Scottish national team and the Ibrox support has changed.

11 Interview with Colin Stein 28/10/01

12 Interview with Colin Stein 28/10/01

13 Interview with Peter McCloy 10/12/01

14 *Glasgow Herald* 20/10/1971 p6 This type of racism, however subconscious, was also displayed in Hugh Taylor's description of 'the dusky Rodrigues' *Daily Record* October 14th 1971.

15 *Glasgow Herald* 22/10/1971 p4

16 *Daily Express* 21/10/1971 p22

17 *Glasgow Herald* 21/10/1971 p22

18 *Daily Record* 21/10/1971 p6

19 *A Bola* 21/10/1971

20 *Jornal de Sporting* 27/10/01

21 *A Bola* 21/10/01

22 *Glasgow Herald* 20/10/1971 p6

23 *Daily Record* 25/10/1971 p22

24 *Glasgow Herald* 25/10/1971 p4

25 There were few fans in Lisbon for the second leg but those who wanted to travel could fly to Lisbon from Prestwick on a 2-day trip with Tollcross Travel, bed and breakfast, airport taxes for the princely sum of £31 – £35 if the hotel was of superior standard (advertised in *Daily Record* 11/10/1971 p5). Of course fans travelling by coach have often had to undertake 24 hour journeys to Europe.

26 *Daily Record* 3/11/1971 p 22

27 *Chronicle* 4/11/71

28 Interview with Peter McCloy 10/12/01

29 Interview with Colin Stein 28/10/01

30 Interview with Alex MacDonald 29/10/01

31 Interview with Colin Stein 28/10/01

32 Interview with Peter McCloy 10/12/01

33 Interview with Willie Johnston, 28/10/01

34 Interview with Sandy Jardine 17/09/01

35 Interview with Sandy Jardine 17/09/01

36 Interview with John Miller 10/10/01

37 Interview with Jack Bain 10/10/01

38 In Sporting's telegram to UEFA, the Portuguese club admit the delegate Andrez Ramirez was aware of the referee's mistake. (see next note)

39 Sporting's telegram gave notice that a letter was being sent with an appeal to the 'Appeal Jury' against the decision, even though the Portuguese had not yet received official confirmation of it. The crux of the arguments to support the appeal were the following points:

(a) Neither club influenced the referee to order penalties to be taken.

The referee gave the result to Sporting after the penalties were taken, and only then did he declare the game as finished.

(b) The decision was public, witnessed by both teams, by the UEFA delegate and by 70,000 spectators.

(c) No appeals were made against the result by anybody from Rangers. An appeal would be essential before the UEFA Organising Committee could make any judgement. (Article 6 of the Rules for the competition)

(d) Rangers had no grounds to appeal because they had agreed to the taking of the penalties.

(e) Because the Organising Committee made a judgement in the absence of any appeal, they broke the letter and the spirit of the rules and therefore their decision should be deemed null and void.

(f) UEFA could not declare Rangers the winners because this would mean ignoring a phase of the game (the penalties) that the referee deemed necessary and without which he did not consider the game finished.

It was absurd for the Committee to substitute itself for the referee, without any appeal from either party, in an area in which the referee should have exclusive competence. This would mean that there are two entities responsible for the running of games.

(g) You cannot divide a game into various parts. The decision of the Committee would lead to the absurd conclusion that a game can be valid up to a certain point and invalid thereafter, which would contradict all the rules of logic, ethics and law. The penalties made up a part of the same game as the referee did not call it finished until after the penalties had been taken.

(h) If the penalties were to be considered null and void, then the whole game would have to be considered null and void. If the penalties were an error made by the referee, then the error called into question the whole game, and not just the extra part (penalties).

(i) The Committee can only confirm or annul the decision of the referee. It cannot change it. In this case, the Committee sought to change the decision of the referee (ie at what point did the game end?). The Committee could only decide that the referee's decision (penalties) was illegal. But given this judgement, then the whole game must be annulled.

Jorge Saraiva, the president of the FPF (Federation Portuguesa de Futebol) also sent a letter to UEFA, supporting Sporting's case. Other points he made were:

(1) The ambiguity of a letter sent to the referee by UEFA before the game (see below).

(2) The coaches and directors of the two teams were unaware of the 'away goals count double in extra time' rule. Indeed, the Scots would not have kept quiet when the ref ordered the penalties if they had known about the rule.

(3) The Scots accepted the result and congratulated the Portuguese. They only went to the Ref's changing room with a copy of the regulations a good quarter of an hour after the game had ended.

(4) UEFA delegate Andre Ramirez realised the mistake that was being made, but by the time he got down to the pitch, the penalties were already under way, and Damas had already saved one. The delegate could not now intervene.

(5) The public and football should not have to pay for the errors of the administrators, referee, directors of the clubs and coaches (who should have known the rules).

The rules had been changed in May '71, so that away goals counted double in extra-time. Before, extra-time was as if it were being played on neutral territory. But UEFA had recently sent a letter to the referee saying the following: 'Please note that the first leg ended in 3-2 in favour of Glasgow Rangers. If the second leg, to be refereed by you, should end with a result of 3-2 in favour of the adversary, extra time of 2x15 will be played after the regulation time is up. If, after this period, the result is still null, the winner will be decided by the taking of penalties.'

40 *Chronicle* 4/11/1971
41 *Chronicle* 4/11/1971
42 *Chronicle* 4/11/1971
43 *Jornal de Sporting* 10/11/1971
44 *Jornal de Sporting* 10/11/1971
45 Thanks to Phil Town (an English football writer who is an expert on Portugese football) who interviewed the former Sporting keeper Dumas and who also translated articles into English.
46 Interview with Sandy Jardine 17/09/01

Torino

1 In the first years of Celtic's nine-in-a-row Championships, Rangers managed to stay within touching distance and were often unlucky not to take the title back to Ibrox. In '66, '67, '68 and '69 Rangers finished the league race in second place and never more than five points behind the champions. In 1969/70, however, while retaining second spot, the losing distance stretched to twelve points. In 1970/71 Rangers slumped to a fourth-place finish and increased the distance between themselves and Jock Stein's side to fifteen points. In 1971/72, Aberdeen were emerging as the only real challengers to Celtic's league domination. In 1972/73 Rangers would finish one point shy of the league title, two seasons later they'd be champions again but in 1971/72 they'd fall a record sixteen points short of the championship – and

Barcelona – here we come!

make the final of neither the League or Scottish Cup. During Celtic's nine-in-a-row era, this season was Rangers' domestic nadir.

2 In 2001/2002 a team had to play a minimum of 13 matches to win the UEFA Cup and 17 to win the Champions League. If a contemporary side were to qualify for the UEFA cup via the Intertoto competition, negotiate the qualifying rounds and then make it all the way to the final as Girodins de Bordeaux did in 1996, they could easily play over 22 matches stretching from July one year to May the next. Incredibly, the Rangers team of 71/72, having defeated Sporting Lisbon in early November would not play another Cup-Winners Cup match till the following March. It was January of 1972 before they even knew which side would become their quarter-final opponents.

3 The Muscovites not only visited Ibrox in the famous 1945 tour but they'd returned in November of 1970 for a friendly match in which Derek Johnstone scored the only goal.

4 And Chelsea it was who allowed Rangers to keep their European engine ticking over during the long winter recess – see note 2, above – when they invited the Ibrox club down to Stamford Bridge in late November for the Ron 'Chopper' Harris testimonial.

5 Widdows, R *Encyclopaedia of World Football* Marshall Cavendish (1980) p173

6 Manna, A & Gibbs, M *The Day Italian Football Died, Torino and the tragedy of Superga* (Breedon 2000) p 140-141

7 Manna, A & Gibbs, M *The Day Italian Football Died, Torino and the tragedy of Superga* (Breedon 2000) p 141

8 Manna, A & Gibbs, M *The Day Italian Football Died, Torino and the tragedy of Superga* (Breedon 2000) p 141-142

9 In 1972 many Rangers supporters would remember the antics of the Fiorentina side which won that historic Cup-Winners' Cup final, first leg, at Ibrox some eleven years previously. Apart from the 'standard' foul play – shirt pulling and diving – there were the unparalleled histrionics which followed the award of a penalty to Rangers. That Rangers legend Eric Caldow missed the spot-kick was unsurprising when even the Fiorentina assistant manager had run onto the field to berate and argue with the Austrian referee, delay matters and generally disturb the concentration and rhythm of the home team.

10 *Daily Record*, 06/03/72 p23

11 *Glasgow Herald* 06/03/72 p4

12 *Glasgow Herald* 08/03/72 p4

13 Interview with Alex MacDonald 29/10/01

14 Torino lost to TSV Munich 1860 in the semi-finals of the 1964/65 European Cup Winners Cup. After a 2-0 win in Italy, they lost 3-1 in Bavaria but, with the away goals rule not yet in force they were forced into a Zurich play-off which the Germans won 2-0. This was perhaps the kind of event which so confused Mr Laurens Van Ravens when he refereed the Rangers v Sporting tie in 1971! Torino eventually reached their first and, so far, only European final in 1992 when they lost the UEFA cup to Ajax . . . on away goals!

15 Interview with Peter McCloy 10/12/01

16 Inglis, S *The Football Grounds of Europe* (Willow 1990) p20-21

17 Inglis, S *The Football Grounds of Europe* (Willow, 1990) p20-21

18 *Glasgow Herald* 09/03/72 p 4

19 Be it through official videos or books, The story of Greig's man-marking duty in the Turin first leg is by now legendary – but it doesn't become any less delicious in the re-telling. Willie Waddell had, as always, equipped the players with pen-

pictures of each member of the Torino team they would be up against. The captain was instructed to 'put Sala out of the game'. Whether Greig was given an actual man-to-man marking job on Sala or simply asked to give him an early spot of 'attention' is unclear and, by now, inconsequential. What is known is that Greig stared at the picture of Torino's international danger man and creator-in-chief with such intensity that it scared even Waddell.

20 Rangers FC Video Production by Cameron Williams: *John Greig, The Legend part 2 1972-1995* (1995)

21 Halliday, S *The Waddell Years 1938-1984* (Chameleon Books 1999) p63

22 *La Stampa* March 9th 1972

23 Interview with Willie Johnston 28/10/01

24 Interview with Colin Stein 28/10/01

25 *Glasgow Herald* 10/03/72 p4

26 *Glasgow Herald* 21/03/72 p4

27 Correspondence from Mauro Ricci

28 Correspondence from Marco Masoero

29 *Glasgow Herald* 22/03/72 p4

30 Interview with Peter McCloy 10/12/01

31 The match kicked-off at 7:30, with a 75,000 all-ticket crowd in their places just half an hour before another 75,000 all-ticket crowd would see the kick-off at Parkhead. That 150,000 people would be watching two games in Glasgow on the same night is perhaps just as unbelievable now as the fact that three European quarter-finalists were that week staying on the Ayrshire coast simultaneously – Rangers in Largs, Celtic. in Seamill and Torino in Troon.

32 Interview with Peter McCloy 10/12/01

33 *Glasgow Herald* 23/03/72 p4

34 Interview with Tommy McLean 19/12/01

35 *La Stampa* March 23 1972

36 Interview with Colin Stein 28/10/01

37 Interview with Willie Johnston 28/10/01

Bayern Munich

1 In the other semi, an all-Eastern Bloc encounter would see a secret policeman's ball between the KGB-bankrolled Dynamo Moscow of the USSR and the Stasi-sponsored Dynamo Berlin of East Germany. The Rangers of Spring 1972 would have gladly risked a trip to either of the communist countries rather than take on the Bundesliga giants.

2 Make no mistake, the huge corporate behemoth which is the Bayern Munich of the 21st century owes all its domestic and international greatness, all its wealth and status to the Bayern Munich of 1972. In fact, it's no exaggeration to say that Germany's present place in the very highest echelons of world footballing history is due more to the players of this club side, in this era than any other before or since.

3 Interesting now to see footage of the game, showing the Bayern fans invading the pitch after the final whistle.

4 The previous season's Fairs Cup, first round encounter had produced a Bayern win but, along with it, the whiff of controversy.

5 Just three days after the joyous and proud night of celebration against Torino, the home league defeat by Morton confirmed, before the month of April, that Rangers would not be winning any league titles in 1972. Only Aberdeen could now stop Celtic from beating their own six-in-a-row record of championships. . . and they were hardly much closer to the reigning champions than Rangers.

6 Interview with Sandy Jardine 17/09/01

7 Nuttelmann, U. *Fazination Bundesliga* (2000) Volume 1 p250

8 Stephen Halliday *The Waddell Years 1938-1984* (Chameleon Books 1999)

9 A former West German youth team coach,

Udo Lattek would later become the first manager in football history to win all three European trophies with different clubs – ironically completing the set in 1982 with a Nou Camp Cup Winners Cup final win as boss of. . . Barcelona!

10 *Glasgow Herald* 05/04/72 p4
11 *Glasgow Herald* 05/04/72 p4
12 *Glasgow Herald* 05/04/72 p4
13 *Glasgow Herald* 05/04/72 p4
14 *Glasgow Herald* 05/04/72 p4
15 Interview with Tommy McLean 19/12/01
16 Interview with Colin Jackson 01/02/02
17 Interview with Colin Stein 28/10/01
18 Interview with Tommy McLean 19/12/01
19 Interview with Sandy Jardine 17/09/01
20 Interview with Colin Stein 28/10/01
21 Interview with Willie Johnston 28/10/01
22 *Glasgow Herald* 06/04/72 p4
23 Nuttelmann, U *Fazination Bundesliga* (2000) Volume 1 p251
24 *Glasgow Herald* 17/04/72 'Old Firm live on TV'
25 *Glasgow Herald* 19/04/72 p4
26 *Glasgow Herald* 19/04/72 p4
27 *Glasgow Herald* 19/04/72 p4
28 It's worth speculating if Waddell's own experience as a player, namely making his debut versus Arsenal at 17 and scoring the only goal of the game, helped him make these choices.
29 Interview with Alex MacDonald 29/10/01
30 Interview with Colin Stein 28/10/01
31 Interview with Colin Jackson 01/02/02
32 Interview with Willie Johnston 28/10/01
33 Interview with Tommy McLean 19/12/01
34 Interview with Billy McMahon 10/10/01
35 Interview with Garry Lynch 17/01/02

The Final
1 Correspondence Sergei Markov 15/09/01
2 Interview with Peter McCloy 10/12/01
3 Interview with Jordi Robisoro 10/09/01
4 Interview with Jack Bain 10/10/01
5 Interview with John Miller 10/10/01
6 Interview with Billy McMahon 10/10/01
7 *Daily Record* 20/05/1972 p7
8 *Daily Express* 18/05/1972 p9
9 *Daily Express* 18/05/1972 p9
10 *Daily Express* 18/05/1972 p9
11 *Daily Express* 19/05/1972 p11
12 *El Correa* 24/05/1972 p27 Thanks to Morag Ramsay for translating this and other Spanish text.
13 *El Correa* 24/05/1972 p27
14 Correspondence Ded Borsov 20/09/01. 'I had also personal impressions of Scotland. At the end of sixties I visited with a trade-union delegation – a great luck at that time. I remember Glasgow very well – unexpectedly cosy city of villas, amusing toy underground, luxurious trade-street, ram's pluck with porridge, blackberry fences and. . . whisky, whisky. I have drunk whisky for all my life – in Aberdeen at a distillery. Free as you can imagine. . . I liked Edinburgh more – castles, history, the spirit of Mary Stuart. . . In Glasgow I begged my hosts to take me to a football match. Celtic – the greens – played, but I do not remember with whom. . . All players seemed red-headed, and a lot of Johnstons were on the pitch. . . And I was struck by the fans – I could not imagine then that it would be "joxes" who will decide the outcome of the memorable final '72. . .'
15 Correspondence Sergei Markov 09/10/01
16 *Daily Express* 23/05/1972 p18
17 Correspondence from British Embassy 09/10/01
18 Interview with Jack Bain 10/10/01
19 Interview with Billy McMahon 10/10/01
20 Correspondence with John Powell 05/01/02
21 Interview with Jim Shirkie 17/01/02
22 Correspondence Sergei Markov 18/09/01
23 Correspondence Didi Borsov 20/09/01
24 Correspondence Sergei Markov 18/09/01

25 Interview with Archie McPherson 06/10/01

26 Interview with Jordi Robisoro 10/09/01

27 *Trud* May 1972

28 Interview with Colin Stein 28/10/01

29 Interview with Archie McPherson 06/10/01

30 Interview with Colin Stein 28/10/01

31 Interview with Alex MacDonald 29/10/01

32 Interview with Alex MacDonald 29/10/01

33 Interview with Colin Jackson 01/02/02

34 *Evening Citizen* 24/05/1972 p5

35 Interview with Willie Johnston 28/10/01

36 Interview with Willie Johnston 28/10/01 Josef Sabo had played in the 1966 World Cup and had actually been a mainstay in the Dynamo Kiev side which won three League titles. After falling foul of officialdom, the midfielder had retired to pursue a career in journalism before eventually making a comeback with Moscow Dynamo at the age of 31. (*World Soccer* December 1971 p9)

37 *Sport Express* 18/10/01

38 Zykov – an interview for the Moscow Dynamo v Rangers programme 01/11/01

39 Interview with Colin Stein 28/10/01

40 Interview with Colin Stein 28/10/01

41 Interview with Willie Johnston 28/10/01

42 Zykov – see 38 above

43 Interview with Willie Johnston 28/10/01

44 *Revista Barcelonista* 30/05/72 Commentator is unnamed

45 Interview with Alex MacDonald 29/10/01

46 Interview with Willie Johnston 28/10/01

47 Zykov – see 38 above

48 Russian electronic newspaper *Gazeta* 2001

49 Interview with Billy McMahon 10/10/01

50 Interview with Archie McPherson 06/10/01

51 Interview with Jordi Robisoro 10/09/01

52 Interview with Colin Glass 04/02/02

53 Correspondence with Ded Borzov 20/09/01 Thanks to Sergei Markov for translating this and all other Russian texts.

54 Interview with Jack Bain 10/10/01

55 Interview with Colin Stein 28/10/01

56 Interview with Peter McCloy 10/12/01

57 Interview with Tommy McLean 19/12/01

58 Interview with Sandy Jardine 17/09/01

59 *Rangers; The Waddell Years* Stephen Halliday (Chameleon Books 1999)

60 Interview with Archie McPherson 06/10/01

61 Jim Craig *A Lion Looks Back* p371 John Donald Publishers 1998

62 Interview with Garry Lynch 17/01/02

'Madness Breaks Out'

1 Interview with Jordi Robisoro 10/09/01

2 Interview with Jack Bain 10/10/01

3 *Daily Express* 26/05/1972 p10

4 *Daily Express* 26/05/1972 p10

5 *Daily Express* 26/05/1972 p10

6 Interview with Archie McPherson

7 Interview with Billy McMahon 10/10/01

8 Interview with Jack Bain 10/10/01

9 Interview with John Miller 10/10/01

10 Correspondence with John Powell 05/01/02

11 See Bill Murray *The Old Firm; Sectarianism and Sport in Scottish Society* (1984) for a fuller discussion on the close relationship between Rangers and the Scottish media. Murray claims that until around the mid sixties the press acted like the PR department of Rangers FC.

12 *Daily Express* 25/05/1972 p1

13 *Daily Record* 25/05/1972 p1

14 *Sunday Mail* 28/05/1972 p32

15 *Glasgow Herald* 25/05/1972 p1

16 *Glasgow Herald* 26/05/1972 p11

17 *El Noticeria* 25/05/1972

18 *El Correa* 26/05/1972

19 *Cronica Madrid* 26/05/1972

20 *El Correa* 26/05/1972

21 *El Correa* 26/05/1972

22 Interview with Billy McMahon 10/10/01

23 A typical example of the post-match reaction can be seen in *Revista Barcelonista* May 30th 1972. Pictures showed the damage Rangers fans created in and around the stadium.

24 *Sunday Telegraph* 13/08/1972

25 *Evening Citizen* 25/05/1972 p5

26 *El Correa* 26/05/72 Yashin said, 'As far as we know the regulations of such tournaments accepted last March by the UEFA, following points of paragraph five of the UEFA decision were violated during the final match.

(Point 16) Nobody without the referee's permission has a right to enter the pitch, such right can be given to coach and medical personnel by a special permission of the referee.

(Point 18) No spectator has a right to appear on the pitch or between the pitch line and the stands.

(Point 20) Necessary numbers of police and stadium administration officers should be present at the match to provide normal situation *(sic)* for the game.

(Point 21) All measures should be taken to prevent spectators appearing on the pitch, if needed the pitch should be protected by a special fence.

This UEFA regulation was signed by the organisation president G Widerker and Secretary General G Bangerter. Both of them were present at the match.

We remember the decision that was taken because of events at a similar match of a European Cup between Inter (Italy) and Borussia (FRG). The situation was much alike. It is known that the above match was replayed. And now we would like to believe in sport fair-play and objective decision of the UEFA commission.'

27 This UEFA regulation was signed by the organisation president Gustav Widerker and Secretary General G Bangerter. Both of them were present at the match.

28 Russian electronic newspaper *Gazeta* 2001: There is a feeling in Russia that UEFA do not deal their sides an even hand. A good example of this occurred earlier in season 2001/2002 when Rangers were allowed to refuse to play in Dagehstan in the UEFA Cup qualifying round. The game was played in neutral Poland.

29 Zykov's interview for the Moscow Dynamo v Rangers programme 01/11/01.

30 The Committee consisted of: Chairman Sergio Zorzi (Switzerland), Aslberto Barbe (Italy), Giuseppe Bonizzi (Malta), Vladimit Tetr (Czechoslovakia), Erkki Poroyla (Finland), Louis Wouters (Belgium).

31 *Glasgow Herald* 25/05/72 p1

32 Interview with Colin Glass 04/02/02

Epilogue

1 Interview with Willie Johnston 28/10/01. Note that it was Waddell who was holding the purse strings although Wallace was in charge of the team.

2 Interview with Colin Stein 28/10/01

3 Interview with Colin Jackson 01/02/02

4 Interview with Colin Glass 04/02/02

5 Quoted in the *Sunday Herald* 13th January 2002. Murray claimed the unsuccessful newspaper the *Sunday Scot* was his other failure.

6 *Down the Copland Road* (Argyll Publishing 2000)

REFERENCES

Books

Craig, J *A Lion looks back* John Donald Publishers Ltd 1998

Esplin, R *Down the Copland Road* Argyll 2000

Fairley, A *Rangers in Europe* Forth Sports Marketing Ltd 1991

Ferrier, B and McElroy, R *Rangers; The Complete Record* Breedon Books 1996

Girault, C; Mislin, G; Hammond, M (Editor: Smith, B) *100 European Cups* Burlington 1992

Glanville, B *Champions of Europe; The history, romance and intrigue of the European Cup* Guinness 1991

Halliday, S *Rangers; The official Illustrated History* Arthur Barker 1989

Halliday, S *Rangers; The Waddell Years 1938 – 1984* Chameleon books 1999

Hockings, R, *Hocking's European Cups* Kenneth Mason publishers 1998

Inglis, S *The Football grounds of Europe* Willow 1990

Lamming, D *A Scottish Internationalist's Who's Who 1872-1986* Hutton Press 1987

McPherson, A *Action Replays* Chapman 1991

Manna, A and Gibbs M *The Day Italian Football Died; Torino and the tragedy of Superga* Breedon 2000

Murray, W *The Old Firm; Sectarianism and Sport in Scotland* John Donald Publshers 1984

Nuttelmann, U *Fazination Bundesliga* 2000

Oliver, G *The Guinness Record of World Soccer* Guinness Publishing 1992

Powter, D (Editor: Robinson, M) *Rangers FC; The 25 Year Record* Soccer Book Publishing Ltd 1995

Radnege, K *The Ultimate Encyclopedia of European Soccer* Ted Smart 1997

Rollin, J *The Rothmans Book of Football Records* Headline Book Publishing 1998

Smailes, G *The Breedon Book of Football Records* Breedon Books 2000

Widows, R *Encyclopedia of World Football* Marshall Cavendish 1980

Scottish newspapers

Daily Record
Daily Express
Evening Times
Evening Citizen
Sunday Mail
Sunday Telegraph
Sunday Herald
Glasgow Herald

Foreign newspapers

Ouest France (France)
A Bola (Portugal)
Chronicle (Portugal)
Jornal de Sporting (Portugal)
La Stampa (Italy)
Trud (Russia)
Gazeta (Russia)
Sport-Express (Russia)
El Correa (Spain)
El Noticeria (Spain)
Revista Barcelonista (Spain)

Miscellaneous

World Soccer 1971
Rangers News
John Greig video *The Legend* Production by Cameron Williams 1995
Rennes centenary magazine *L'Histoire du Stade Rennais 100 ans en Rouge et Noir* 2001

RANGERS' EUROPEAN RECORD TO 1971/72

Scottish involvement in European football began not with the League or Cup winners but with Hibernian's talented side of the 1950s which represented Scotland in the inaugral European Cup in 1955/56. The Edinburgh men were put out in the semi finals by French side Rheims. The tournament immediately transformed itself and the next season only national champions were invited into the European Cup proper.

European Cup 1956/57
Having won the Scottish championship in 1955/56 Rangers duly took their place amongst Europe's elite.
1st Round 1st Leg; 24th October 1956 Rangers 2 Nice 1
2nd Leg; 14th November 1956 Nice 2 Rangers 1
Rangers large home crowd of 65,000 was in stark contrast to Nice where only 5000 locals turned up. Clearly European football had still to catch on in France.
1st Round Play off lay (in Paris) 28th November 1956
Rangers 1 OGC Nice 3 (a curious neutral venue)

European Cup 1957/58
The early Euro setback in 56/57 never rattled Rangers in terms of domestic form and they once again won the league that season. So it was their second campaign in the European Cup and once again French opponents figured.
1st Round 1st leg; September 4th 1957
Rangers 3 St Etienne 1
2nd leg; September 25th 1957 St Etienne 2 Rangers 1

2nd Round, 1st leg; November 27th 1957
Rangers 1 AC Milan 4
2nd leg; December 11th 1957 AC Milan 2 Rangers 0

European Cup 1959/60
Rangers failed to win the league in 1957/58 and dropped out of European competition for a season but when they regained the title in 1958/59 it was back into the fray. Popularity and interest in the European Cup was growing and a preliminary round was introduced which the Scottish representatives found themselves in.
Preliminary round 1st leg; September 16th 1959
Rangers 5 Anderlecht 2
Preliminary round 2nd leg; September 23rd 1959
Anderlecht 0 Rangers 2

1st Round 1st leg November 11th 1959
Rangers 4 Red Star Bratislava 3
2nd leg; November 18th 1959
Red Star Bratislava 1 Rangers 1

2nd Round 1st leg; March 9th 1960
Sparta Rotterdam 2 Rangers 3
2nd leg; March 16th 1960 Rangers 0 Sparta Rotterdam 1
2nd Round play-off March 30th 1960
Rangers 3 Sparta Rotterdam 2 (at Highbury)

Semi Final 1st leg; April 13 1960
Eintracht Frankfurt 6 Rangers 1
2nd leg; May 5th 1960 Rangers 3 Eintrach Frankfurt 6

European Cup Winners Cup 1960/61
At that point the popularity of European football resulted in a third competition being formatted and the European Cup Winners Cup was born. Hearts had won the championship for the second time in three seasons so Rangers' Scottish Cup victory over Kilmarnock meant the Ibrox club were offered a chance to compete in European football again.
1st Round 1st leg; September 28th 1960
Rangers 4 Ferencvaros 2
2nd leg; October 12th 1960 Ferencvaros 2 Rangers 1

2nd Round 1st leg; November 15th 1960
Borussia Monchengladbach 0 Rangers 3
2nd leg; November 30th 1960
Rangers 8 Borussia Monchengladbach 0

Semi Final 1st leg; March 29th 1961 Rangers 2 Wolves 0
2nd Leg; April 19th 1961 Wolves 1 Rangers 1

Final 1st leg; May 17th 1961 Rangers 0 Fiorentina 2
2nd leg; May 27th 1961 Fiorentina 2 Rangers 1

European Cup 1961/62
Unlucky for Rangers but their championship win meant yet
another go at the top tournament.
1st Round 1st leg; September 5th 1961
 AS Monaco 2 Rangers 3
2nd leg; September 12th 1961 Rangers 3 AS Monaco 2

2nd Round 1st leg; November 15th 1961
AEK Vorwaerts 1 Rangers 2
2nd leg; November 22nd 1961 Rangers 1 AEK Vorwaerts 0
(In Malmo, abandoned after 45 mins)
2nd leg; rearranged November 23rd 1961
Rangers 4 Vorwaerts 1

Quarter Final 1st Leg; February 7th 1962
Standard Liege 4 Rangers 1
Quarter Final 2nd leg; February 14th 1962
Rangers 2 Standard Liege 0

European Cup Winners Cup 1962/63
With Dundee winning the league in 1961/62 season Rangers
had to be content with a European Cup Winners Cup place
courtesy of a Scottish Cup win over St Mirren.
1st Round 1st leg; September 5th 1962 Rangers 4 Seville 0
2nd leg; September 26th 1962 Seville 2 Rangers 0

2nd round 1st leg; October 31st 1962 Spurs 5 Rangers 2
2nd leg; December 11th 1962 Rangers 2 Spurs 3

European Cup 1963/64
With the league championship regained in 62/63 it was back
into the European Cup for the next season. This was one of
Rangers best ever teams but they suffered an almighty
thrashing at the hands of the European masters Real Madrid.
1st Round 1st leg; September 25th 1963
Rangers 0 Real Madrid 1
2nd leg; October 9th 1963 Real Madrid 6 Rangers 0

European Cup 1964/65
Despite that early exit at the hands of Madrid Rangers were
still top dogs in Scotland, winning the league again and
another chance the following season proved more fruitful.
1st Round 1st leg; September 2nd 1964
Rangers 3 Red Star Belgrade 1
1st Round 2nd leg; September 9th 1964
Red Star Belgrade 4 Rangers 2
1st round play off; November 4th 1964
Rangers 3 Red Star Belgrade 1 (at Highbury)

2nd Round 1st leg; November 18th 1964
Rangers 1 Rapid Vienna 0
2nd leg; December 8th 1964 Rapid Vienna 0 Rangers 2

3rd Round 1st leg; February 17th 1965 Inter Milan 3 Rangers 1
2nd leg; March 3rd 1965 Rangers 1 Inter Milan 0

European Cup Winners Cup 1966/67
Celtic won the league in season 65/66 for the first time since
1953/54 and it was to prove significant in that Rangers' rivals
went on to win the European Cup at the first time of asking.
Rangers themselves got to the final of the European Cup
Winners Cup a week later but once again failed at the final
hurdle. It was a week that changed the football world for both
sides.
1st Round 1st leg; September 27th 1966 Glentoran 1 Rangers 1
2nd leg; October 5th 1966 Rangers 4 Glentoran 0

2nd Round 1st leg; November 23rd 1966
Rangers 2 Borussia Dortmund 1
2nd leg; December 6th 1966 Borussia Dortmund 0 Rangers 0

3rd Round 1st leg; March 1st 1967
Rangers 2 Real Zaragossa 0
2nd leg; March 22nd 1967 Real Zaragossa 2 Rangers 0
(After extra time, Rangers won on the toss of the coin)

Semi Final 1st leg; April 19th 1967 Slavia Sofia 0 Rangers 1
2nd leg; May 3rd 1967 Rangers 1 Slavia Sofia 0

May 31st 1967 Final in Nuremberg, West Germany
Rangers 0 Bayern Munich 1 (After extra time)

Barcelona – here we come!

Inter Cities Fairs Cup 1967/68

Celtic went on to win all the trophies they competed for in 1966/67 and their subsequent nine in a row run meant there was to be no European Cup participation for the Ibrox men until 1975/76 season. Beaten Scottish Cup finalists Aberdeen entered the Cup Winners Cup and the Ibrox club had to be content with entry into the European Inter Cities Fairs Cup, the forerunner of the UEFA Cup.

1st Round 1st leg; September 20th 1967
Dynamo Dresden 1 Rangers 1
2nd leg; October 4th 1967 Rangers 2 Dynamo Dresden 1

1967 2nd Round 1st leg; November 8th Rangers 3 Cologne 0
2nd leg; November 28th 1967 Cologne 3 Rangers 1 (after extra time)

Quarter Final 1st leg; March 26th 1968 Rangers 0 Leeds United 0
2nd leg; April 9th 1968 Leeds United 2 Rangers 0

Inter Cities Fairs Cup 1968/69

Trophyless again in season 67/68 it was the Inter Cities Fairs Cup once more for the Ibrox men and there was an ominous fracas at Newcastle which, although there had previously been trouble in Wolverhampton and London, became the first high profile bout of hooliganism.

1st Round 1st leg; September 18th 1968
Rangers 2 Vojvidina 0
2nd leg; October 2nd 1968 Vojvidina 1 Rangers 0

2nd Round 1st leg; October 30th 1968 Rangers 6 Dundalk 1
2nd leg; November 13th 1968 Dundalk 0 Rangers 3

3rd Round 1st leg; January 15th 1969
DWS Amsterdam 0 Rangers 2
2nd leg; January 22nd 1969 Rangers 2 DWS Amsterdam 1

Quarter Final 1st leg; March 19th 1969
Rangers 4 Atletico Madrid 1
2nd leg; April 2nd 1969 Atletico Madrid 2 Rangers 0

Semi Final 1st leg; May 14th 1969 Rangers 0 Newcastle 0
2nd leg; May 21st 1969 Newcastle 2 Rangers 0

European Cup Winners Cup 1969/70

Celtic won their fourth Championship in a row 68/69 so Rangers' participation in the European Cup Winners Cup was as a result of the infamous 4-0 drubbing at the hands of their rivals in the Scottish Cup Final. Not the most glorious way to qualify for any European competition and indeed it was something of a turbulent time for the Ibrox club struggling to come to terms with the Celtic revival.

1st Round 1st leg; September 17th 1969
Rangers 2 Steau Bucharest 0
2nd leg; October 1st 1969 Steau Bucharest 0 Rangers 0

2nd Round 1st leg; November 12th 1969
Gornik Zabrze 3 Rangers 1
2nd leg; November 26th 1969 Rangers 1 Gornik Zabrze 3

Inter Cities Fairs Cup 1970/71

It was back to the Inter City Fairs Cup where once again Rangers found themselves facing the Bayern side who were beginning to make their mark on the European scene.

1st Round 1st leg; September 16th 1970
Bayern Munich 1 Rangers 0
2nd leg; September 30th 1970 Rangers 1 Bayern Munich 1

Rangers European record prior to the 1971/72 season had been solid and consistent and Scottish football was regarded with some respect throughout Europe. Only 15 teams have competed for Scotland in Europe and of those who have made any sort of impact, the majority did so in the 1960s. Celtic of course had won the European Cup in 1967 and were beaten finalists in 1970 as well as reaching the semi finals of the Cup Winners Cup in 1965. Dundee had reached the semi finals of the European Cup in 1962/63 and the semi finals of the Fairs Cup in 1967/68. Dunfermline had reached the quarter finals of the Cup Winners Cup in 1961/62 and the same stage of the Fairs Cup in 1965/66 before going to the semi finals of the Cup Winners Cup in season 1968/69. Hibs of course had reached the semi final of the inaugral European Competition, the semi final of the Fairs Cup in 1960/61 and also the quarter finals in 1962/63. Kilmarnock had reached the semi finals of the Fairs Cup in 1966/67.

OTHER BOOKS FROM ARGYLL PUBLISHING

Down the
Copland Road

RONNIE ESPLIN

1 902831 14 4 192pages £7.99

Down the Copland Road gives space to that traditionally important section of every top professional football club – its supporters. Author and freelance football writer Ronnie Esplin tackles supporters' views on the commercialisation of football, about where to now in Scotland, and what an increasingly European focus holds for Rangers FC.

Rangers fans reflect on their reputation and speak out on the religious, political and media profile of the club and its followers. **Down the Copland Road** takes a look at the highs and lows of following the team and is a must for football fans everywhere.

"hard to resist"
Sunday Herald

"provocative, compelling and authentic"
The Herald

"a hard hitting look at life following the Bears"
Rangers News

"comprehensive"
Scottish Memories

"a far reaching survey of the followers of Scotland's leading club"
Sunday Post

"Ronnie Esplin has rendered Rangers and their fans a great service"
Bill Murray

Available from bookshops and Argyll Publishing 01369 820229 Post Free in UK